Uncle John's
BATHROOM READER.

BATHROOM READERS' PRESS
ASHLAND, OREGON

"I don't believe in accidents. There are only encounters in history. There are no accidents."

—**Pablo Picasso**

"We are glade to pre-approve you for a Educaiton Degree!"

—**a spam text message received by Uncle John while working on this book**

UNCLE JOHN'S BATHROOM READER®
ZIPPER ACCIDENTS

"Bathroom Reader," "Portable Press," and "Bathroom Readers' Institute"
are registered trademarks of Baker & Taylor. All rights reserved.

For information, write: The Bathroom Readers' Institute,
P.O. Box 1117, Ashland, OR 97520
www.bathroomreader.com

Cover and interior design by Andy Taray / Ohioboy.com

Library of Congress Cataloging-in-Publication Data

Uncle John's bathroom reader zipper accidents.

pages cm

ISBN 978-1-60710-778-1 (pbk.)

1. American wit and humor. 2. Curiosities and wonders. I. Bathroom
Readers' Institute (Ashland, Or.) II. Title: Zipper accidents.

PN6165.U5296 2013

081—dc23

2012045784

Printed in the United States of America
First Printing: April 2013
1 2 3 4 5   17 16 15 14 13

THANK YOU!

The Bathroom Readers' Institute sincerely thanks the people whose advice and assistance made this book possible.

Gordon Javna
Brian Boone
Andy Taray
Christy Taray
Trina Janssen
Claudia Bauer
Jay Newman
Thom Little
Dan Mansfield
Brandon Hartley
Megan Todd
Eleanor Pierce
Michael Conover
Jill Bellrose
Kim Griswell
David Hoye
Jennifer Frederick
Sydney Stanley
Lilian Nordland
Melinda Allman
JoAnn Padgett
Aaron Guzman
Gideon Sundback

CONTENTS

BABY
ON
BOARD

ZIPPER ACCIDENTS

ACCIDENTS WILL HAPPEN!

Let's face it: Life is hard. Everyday you're forced to wake up and do a whole bunch of things. *Thousands* of things. Most are relatively simple, like breathing or finding a pair of matching socks. But too many of these tasks are fraught with peril: pulling out of your driveway, merging into traffic, and trying to do so while texting, for example. (Also: finding a pair of matching socks.)

So it goes.

Thing after thing after thing must be done, and you're not allowed to screw up even one of those! But, inevitably, you do. We all do. Thankfully, most errors go unnoticed. But some people's goofs make the evening news. Or the history books. It's then that these little moments of embarrassment get shared the world over, leading all of us to look on, shake our heads and remark, "What a shame," and then "I'm sure glad that wasn't me."

That's what *Zipper Accidents* is all about: We call out the all-time biggest screw-ups...so you can feel better about yourself. Consider it our gift. So happy reading...and don't forget to look where you're driving while you do.

—Uncle John and the Bathroom Readers' Institute

LOTTO-NO

An elderly English woman purchased a EuroMillions lottery form in 2010, brought it home, picked her numbers, and gave it to her husband to turn in. And, as she always did, she wrote down her numbers on a piece of paper. A few days later came the big announcement—all her numbers were drawn! She'd won! One problem: Her husband had tossed the ticket into the garbage bin. The couple would have won £113 million ($181 million).

• Martyn and Kay Tott bought a National Lottery ticket in England in 2001. Watching the news a few nights later, they heard that the jackpot of £3 million was still unclaimed. Then the newsreader delivered the numbers, and they were the numbers the Totts always played. The couple, celebrating their first wedding anniversary, were thrilled and poked around for their ticket to millions—but they couldn't find it. Ultimately, the 30-day time limit on lost tickets claims came and went. Three lengthy legal battles ensued; the Totts won none of them. The stress over the gain—and immediate loss—of millions strained their marriage, and the couple split.

UN-LIMB-ITED

Fifty-one-year-old William King was in a Tampa, Florida, hospital in 1995 for the amputation of his right foot, which had became gangrenous due to complications from adult-onset diabetes. Just before he went under the anesthesia, he joked with medical staff, "Make sure you don't take the wrong one." Guess what happened? The doctors amputated his healthy left foot, and spared him the gangrenous right one.

King ultimately had to have *both* legs amputated below the knee, and he received a hefty settlement. The hospital where the mix-up occurred, University Community Hospital, instituted a new practice to ensure the same mistake wasn't repeated: A medical professional had to write "NO" on all limbs not slated for amputation. This procedure, simple yet amazingly effective, has been adopted at thousands of hospitals around the world.

> ## "THE DOCTORS AMPUTATED HIS HEALTHY LEFT FOOT, AND SPARED HIM THE GANGRENOUS RIGHT ONE.""

IF THE U.S. WINS, YOU WIN & McDONALD'S LOSES

Patriotism surges before and during the Olympics, especially when the Olympics are on home soil. That was the climate in 1984 as the Los Angeles Summer Games approached. McDonald's capitalized on America's Olympic fever with a massive promotion called "If the U.S. wins, you win!" Whenever a customer bought certain food items, they received a scratch-off game piece emblazoned with an Olympic event—if an American won a medal in that event, the customer won a Big Mac (for a gold), fries (for silver), or a soda (bronze). McDonald's wasn't worried about having to give away too much free stuff because in the 1976 Olympics, the U.S. won 94 medals; the Soviet Union won 125 and East Germany won 90.

But then, just weeks before the Games were to begin, the USSR announced a Communist boycott of the 1984 Olympics as payback for the U.S.-led 1980 boycott. The USSR sat out, as did traditional powerhouses like East Germany, Hungary, Czechoslovakia, and Poland. With its major foes out of the way, the U.S. had a much clearer path to Olympic glory, and made good on it, winning an astounding 174 medals, 83 of them gold. The U.S. won, consumers won, but the big loser was McDonald's, which lost tens of millions giving away food it didn't think it was going to have to give away.

DETHY'S DEATHTRAP

Louis Dethy was a 79-year-old retired man living in Charlerois, Belgium, in 2002. He lived alone, having alienated his large family—his wife and 14 children—through infidelity and refusing to forgive *them* for not forgiving him. In 1998 he lost a legal battle over his mother's will, which left Dethy's house (which she had owned) to one of his daughters. Essentially facing eviction from a family he had come to see as the enemy, Dethy decided to booby-trap his house—if he couldn't keep it, he'd kill them all before he let them have it. He hid 20 shotguns around the house that would fire if triggered: one over a crate of beer bottles that would set the gun off when emptied, one on a chest full of cash in the cellar, one on a water tank, and even one on the TV. To make sure he didn't shoot himself first, Dethy wrote himself tons of coded notes and riddles and stashed those around the house, too. Nonetheless, Dethy accidentally set off one of the guns and shot himself. A military mine-clearance team had to be called in to rid the house of the other 19 firearms... and Dethy's body.

"DETHY DECIDED TO BOOBY-TRAP HIS HOUSE—IF HE COULDN'T KEEP IT, HE'D KILL THEM ALL BEFORE HE LET THEM HAVE IT."

GRIEVOUS BODILY HARM

A shocking development. Michael Anderson Godwin was convicted of murder in South Carolina in 1989. Somehow, he avoided the electric chair and got life in prison instead. Then one day, while sitting on a steel toilet in his cell, he was trying to repair a pair of headphones...while they were plugged in. He electrocuted himself and died.

If at first you don't succeed... An unnamed 30-year-old man in Kent, New York, attempted suicide by jumping out of a fourth-story window of an apartment building. But he landed on a parked car and survived. When he recovered, he tried again, jumping out the same window. He landed on the same car and fractured his ankle and wrist.

Mr. Clean. When police found 18-year-old Michael Smeriglio of Port St. Lucie, Florida, he was in bad shape. There was a lot of blood... down there. Smeriglio told the cops he'd been shot by hoodlums. But he was lying. He was cleaning his gun when it fired. According to press reports, "The bullet went through his penis, his left testicle, and then lodged itself in his thigh."

That bites. Illinois Baptist minister Paul Wrenn performs tremendous feats of strength to demonstrate the power of faith, like pounding nails into boards with his bare hands, or letting parishioners jump on his stomach. At a 1988 service, he lifted a 385-pound man a few inches off the ground with his teeth, using a special mouthpiece. Then the mouthpiece slipped, immediately tearing five teeth out of Wrenn's mouth, each of them reportedly left dangling by a nerve. Wrenn put the large man down, finished his sermon, then sought medical attention.

Burns's burn. In 2012, a drug cop, unnamed in press reports, completed a home search in Mercer Island, Washington. When he went to re-holster his gun, it fired. According to Mercer Island police commander Leslie Burns, "He did shoot his buttocks area, but he'll be fine." No word on the extent of injuries to his ego area.

It could have been any red, octagonal sign. Police in St. Augustine, Florida, pulled over Leslie Richard Newton, 63, when they spotted him driving his Chevy Camaro erratically. Earlier on his joy ride, Newton had blasted through a stop sign. As in, he blasted through the sign itself, destroying it. Then he kept on driving. The reason the accident made news: Newton still had a chunk of the stop sign embedded in his skull when he was pulled over. According to reports, "Alcohol was a factor."

A MINOR DETAIL, REALLY

JUST ONE PAIR OF BINOCULARS. David Blair, the original second officer on the *Titanic*, was relieved of duty shortly before the ship set off for New York on April 10, 1912. In Blair's haste to leave, he forgot to turn over all of his equipment to his replacement. One of the forgotten items was the key to the crow's nest telephone. Blair had also left the crow's nest binoculars in his cabin. According to the testimony of surviving crew members, if the lookouts had been given the binoculars, they would have seen the iceberg sooner. And if they'd had access to the phone, they could have alerted the bridge sooner. Either scenario might well have given the *Titanic* enough time to safely change course.

JUST A MATTER OF DISTRIBUTION. In 1965 journalist Lionel Burleigh announced that he was starting a brand-new newspaper to serve London, the *Commonwealth Sentinel*. He promised nonbiased reporting and truth telling, renting billboards to announce his paper as "Britain's most fearless newspaper." The first issue came out on February 6, 1965. That was the last issue.

> "EITHER SCENARIO MIGHT WELL HAVE GIVEN THE *TITANIC* ENOUGH TIME TO SAFELY CHANGE COURSE."

Spending all of his time writing articles, collecting ads, and getting the paper to press, Burleigh had neglected to arrange distribution. The first edition's 50,000 copies were dumped outside the hotel where he was staying. By the time the matter was sorted out, the news in the paper was old news. The paper folded, having sold one issue, by Burleigh's daughter to a pedestrian walking by the hotel.

JUST ONE PEDAL OVER. In 1971 Helen Ireland of Auburn, California, got into her car to take her driver's license test. She said good morning to the tester, started the engine, then pressed down on the accelerator instead of the clutch and drove straight through the DMV's wall. Total time of driving test: about one second. (She didn't pass.)

JUST ONE CONVERSION ERROR. It was a case of the left hand not knowing what the right hand was doing. NASA's Jet Propulsion Laboratory was the left hand; they used metric units in their calculations while designing the Mars Climate Orbiter. Aerospace company Lockheed Martin was the right hand; they used the customary feet and inches. Then, nine months and 461 million miles after it launched in December 1998, the mismatched figures caused the orbiter's space brakes to not fire in time. The craft, which weighed 750 pounds (or, if you prefer, 340 kilograms), hit the Martian atmosphere at the wrong angle and was never heard from again. Cost of the mission: $327 million.

BUSINESS BLUNDERS

I n 1963 an eight-year-old West Virginia girl ate her box of Cracker Jack, and then got to her "free surprise" inside: a booklet called "Erotic Sexual Positions from Around the World." Cracker Jack manufacturer Borden said that six books in all were found around the U.S., and attributed them to "an individual with a very sick sense of humor."

• **There are thousands of apps for Apple's iPhone,** but none has drawn more complaints than the "Baby Shaker": a video game in which the player shakes the iPhone until a virtual baby stops crying (then two red X's appear over its eyes). The app was available for download for just two days in 2009 before Apple removed it. The company explained that it should have been rejected before it was added, but someone must have "missed it." Alex Talbot, the app's designer, admitted, "Yes, the Baby Shaker was a bad idea."

• **Potato-chip company Walkers** held a contest in 2010 that awarded prize money to customers who accurately predicted the weather. Entrants had to buy a 65-cent pack of Walkers chips, then, using the two game pieces in

the bag, go to the company's website and predict when and where in the country it would rain. If they did so correctly, they won about $16. What went wrong? Walkers is an extremely popular brand of snacks in England, where it rains *a lot*. And the contest was held in the fall, when it *really* rains a lot. As far as weather statistics in England go, contestants had a better than 1-in-3 chance of predicting a rainy day. Finally, when an especially rainy week was set to occur, Walkers took the contest website down with no warning.

• **In 1983, Paul McCartney collaborated with Michael Jackson** on a song called "Say, Say, Say," which would ultimately become a #2 hit. At the time, Jackson was at the peak of his fame, with his *Thriller* album selling as many as a million copies a week. On the set of the video for their hit single "Say, Say, Say," Jackson asked McCartney, ludicrously wealthy as a Beatle and successful solo artist, for tips on how to manage his newfound wealth. McCartney told him that the real money in music is in publishing—buying the rights to popular songs. Whenever those songs get played on the radio or used in movies or TV commercials, the owner of the publishing rights gets a cut. Good idea, thought Jackson. So in 1984, when Associated Television Corporation's catalog of 4,000 songs went on sale, Jackson bought it for $47.5 million. Among those songs? Most Beatles songs.

SODA JERKS

The staff at a Family Dollar store in Kansas City, Missouri, were having trouble with a food thief—one of the employees would routinely steal others' food and drinks out of a staff refrigerator and consume them. To teach him a lesson, the store's assistant manager dropped a total of 50 dissolving laxative tablets into two 20-ounce bottles of Coca-Cola, then resealed the bottles with glue to make them look unopened, then put them in the staff fridge, knowing the food thief would have his way with them...and get a nasty surprise (eventually).

The target of the prank, however, noticed the undissolved tablets in the Cokes (there were a lot of tablets, after all) and decided to pull a prank of his own—he put the bottles with the Cokes in a cooler on the sales floor, where customers can buy them. Later that day, a 54-year-old woman bought one of the Cokes and drank some before noticing the laxative residue in the bottle. She returned to the Family Dollar to complain, and while doing so, became violently ill in the way that consuming more than a dozen laxative pills can do. She had to be hospitalized, and even though Family Dollar's corporate office called her to apologize and offered her a $200 gift card, she sued the store. Both employees involved were fired and arrested.

CIVIC ERRORS

A work crew was sent to dredge a clogged canal in Nottinghamshire, England, in 1978. In just a few hours they pulled out all of the household waste local residents had thrown in, such as rusted car parts, old appliances, even a heavy chain attached to a large wooden block. The crew then took a break for tea time. That's when a resident noticed that the canal water was violently swirling around, and that the water level was quickly dropping. The work crew had removed the canal's plug. In just a few minutes, the mile-and-a-half-long canal had drained into the river.

• **In a Ventura, California, parade,** a drum major threw a baton high into the air, where it struck a power line. It shorted out, leading to a 10-block power outage, putting a radio station off the air, and started a grass fire.

• **In 1992 the Greenville, South Carolina,** Department of Social Services sent out this letter to a deceased food stamp recipient: "Your food stamps will be stopped because we received notice that you passed away. You may reapply if there is a change in your circumstances."

THE INFLATABLE TRUCKER

In May 2011, New Zealand truck driver Steven McCormack was cleaning his truck at his company's workshop in Whakatane, on the east coast of the country's North Island. McCormack was standing on the rigging between his truck's cab and trailer when he slipped. As he began to fall, he knocked a high-pressure air-brake hose of its nozzle. When he landed, that pointy brass nozzle—which was releasing air at 120 pounds per square inch—punctured McCormack's skin, right in his butt.

McCormack's body immediately began to inflate. "His body started to literally blow up!" McCormack's boss, Robbie Petersen, who witnessed the accident, told reporters afterward. "Before we knew it, his face went up like a balloon!" McCormack's butt was stuck to the nozzle for more than a minute before a coworker finally hit a safety valve that shut the air off. By that time, McCormack's body had inflated to twice its normal size—and he was screaming in agony.

Someone called 111 (New Zealand's 911). Both of the small town's two ambulances were busy, and a rescue helicopter was on a mission more than two hours away. So coworkers lifted McCormack off the nozzle and laid him down on the ground. They placed ice packs around the wound and also around his neck, which was dangerously puffed up with air. ("I felt like the Michelin Man," McCormack said later.) It took an hour for paramedics to arrive.

Doctors said McCormack was lucky to have survived the freak accident. The high-pressure air had filled and swollen his buttocks and legs as well as his abdomen and chest—dangerously compressing his heart and lungs. Air had even collected behind McCormack's eyeballs. Doctors also said that the air had separated muscle from fat in various places around McCormack's body, and that they were surprised it didn't rupture his skin.

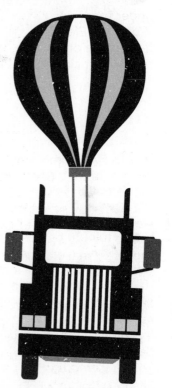

But in the end, all was well: McCormack was out of the hospital in a couple of days and back to work in a few of weeks. And all that extra air in his body? It left the natural way— via burps and farts.

THREE ELECTION GAFFES

Good joke. Comic Jacob Haugaard ran for the Danish parliament in 1994. He ran under the Union of Conscientiously Work-Shy Elements party, of which he was the only member. Campaign promises included better weather, shorter lines in stores, and other things out of his control, satirizing campaign promises. And yet, he got more than 23,000 votes...enough for a seat in the parliament.

Did I forget something? Herbert Connolly had to campaign hard to retain his seat on the Massachusetts Governor's Council in 1988. He did "Get out the vote" activities all day on Election Day. He worked so hard that he lost track of the time and got to his precinct to vote for himself, 15 minutes too late. Final election results: 14,715 to 14,716—in his opponent's favor.

Decline of the machines. In 2007 Domenic Volpe ran for the Virginia legislature. His campaign used "robocall" machines to deliver campaign messages. Most find these annoying at any time, but Volpe's campaign inadvertently set the machines to make the calls at 2 a.m. Had he not alienated hundreds, he may have won the election.

CELEBRITY MARRIAGE WEIRDNESS

During production on *The Ben Stiller Show* in 1992, cast member Janeane Garofalo and writer Rob Cohen were dating. On a trip to Las Vegas, they got drunk and got married at one of the city's many drive-through chapels. They thought the marriage wasn't real. "We thought you have to go to the downtown courthouse and sign papers and stuff," Garofalo later recalled. The couple split up a few months after. Garofalo became a major comedian, while Cohen went on to produce and write for *The Big Bang Theory*. In 2012 he proposed to his girlfriend. Only then, when Cohen's lawyer was getting his records in order, did Garofalo and Cohen realize they had actually been legally married in 1992... and still were. Garofalo and Cohen amicably re-united and divorced a few weeks later.

• Actor Ryan O'Neal was the longtime companion of actress Farrah Fawcett. Moments after Faw-cett's funeral in 2009, O'Neal was taken aback when "a beautiful blond" came up and hugged him. Despite having just put the love of his life in the ground, O'Neal asked the woman if she wanted to go get a drink. "Daddy, it's me," replied actress Tatum O'Neal, his estranged daughter.

ONE FALSE STROKE

SPELL CZECH
The town council for the British town of Kirklees decided to promote itself and the surroundings as the ideal hamlet for bicycling. However, before printing up more than 7,000 brochures, nobody noticed some major spelling mistakes. "Cleckheaton" was misspelled as "Czechisation," "Birstall" became "Bistable," "Kirkburton" became "Kirkpatrick," and even "Kirklees" became "Kirtles." An e-mail address for British Waterways was listed as the wildly inaccurate "enquiries.manic-depressive@brutalisation's.co.uk." A council spokesman blamed the errors on the printer's software.

UNLIKE
In 2009, when Sir John Sawer was appointed head of MI6, the British government's spy agency, his wife, Shelley, posted the good news on her Facebook page. Unfortunately, Mrs. Sawer hadn't enabled any of the social networking site's privacy features, meaning that anyone with Internet access could see her page, which contained sensitive information about her and her husband, including where they lived, places they frequently visited, and photos of their children. After the leak was discovered, Mrs. Sawer hastily made her Facebook page accessible to friends only.

ZOO, SCREW, SUE

In 2001 Marguerite Nunn intended to donate a $130 check to Zoo to You, a nonprofit wildlife education program. But due to what was later deemed a "software error" on her computer, her zip code was entered into the amount box on the check. Result: She donated $93,447. When Nunn, an innkeeper from Paso Robles, California, realized the error two weeks later, she asked for Zoo to You to return her money. But they'd already spent more than half of it. (The check had cleared the bank because Nunn and her husband, Tom, had recently sold some property and deposited the proceeds.) The nonprofit paid back $30,000, and then a little more over the next few years, but nothing came after 2006. Seeing no other choice, the Nunns sued. In 2009, they were awarded a settlement reported as "somewhere in the middle."

JUST SAY NO

The Florida House of Representatives voted down a law to widen government-paid health services in 1990. The bill was rejected by a single vote, that of Representative Mike Langton. Or, more accurately, of his 12-year-old son. Langton stepped away to make a phone call, leaving the boy to play at his desk on the House floor. The bill came up for a vote, and the younger Langton fiddled around with the electronic voting device and accidentally cast a no vote. The elder Langton had intended to vote yes.

THE ROGUE TRADER

I n 1992 a British commodities trader named Nick Leeson moved to Singapore to manage futures markets for Barings Bank, the oldest merchant bank in the United Kingdom. Leeson, then only in his mid-20s, was given a great deal of responsibility—and a salary to match—by the bank, and lived it up in Singapore. Leeson was banned from a fancy cricket club for shouting a racial slur. He also spent a night in jail after a booze-fueled mooning spree.

Eager to fund his increasingly lavish lifestyle, Leeson began making risky investments on behalf of Barings. Initially, they paid off, netting him a large bonus on top of his annual salary because he earned millions for the bank. Then his luck changed. As his losses began to mount, he attempted to hide them in an "error account" (which are typically used by traders to correct mistakes) which he labeled "88888" (8 is a lucky number in Chinese numerology). Now a chief trader with Barings, Leeson exploited his new title to conceal a rapidly expanding negative cash flow.

At the end of 1992, the error account contained £2 million (about $1.32 million) worth of Leeson's mistakes. That amount blazed to an astonishing £208 million ($137 million) by Christmas 1994. The young trader's house of cards came crashing down when he made a series of overly optimistic bets on the Japanese stock market on January 16, 1995. An earthquake struck Kobe the following morning, sending markets across Asia, and Leeson's investments, into a tailspin. Leeson fled.

"THERE WAS NO WAY THE BANK COULD COVER HIS LOSSES OF $1.3 BILLION."

Leeson's carelessness quickly brought Barings to the brink of collapse. There was no way the bank could cover his losses of $1.3 billion. While the media began predicting the imminent demise of the bank, an international manhunt was on. Rumor hounds speculated that Leeson had zoomed off to another Asian nation or that he was sailing the high seas on a private yacht. Actually, he was holed up at the five-star Regent Hotel in Kuala Lumpur. Leeson and his wife later attempted to flee to Britain, but he was nabbed at the Frankfurt Airport in Germany on March 2.

By then, Barings had been declared insolvent. It was eventually sold to ING, a Dutch banking and insurance firm, for the meager sum of a single pound, bringing a somber end to more than 230 years of banking history.

Leeson spent more than three and a half years in a Singapore prison but was released in 1999 after being diagnosed with colon cancer. Leeson eventually bounced back. He managed to beat cancer, remarried, and these days he lectures at business conventions on the topic of "corporate responsibility."

ZERO TOLERANCE

Feet 'n' meat. Kaylin Frederich went into a Burger King in Sunset Hills, Missouri, with two relatives in August 2009. After the family had started eating, an employee told them that they had to leave—because Kaylin wasn't wearing shoes, a violation of the restaurant's "no shoes, no shirt, no service" policy. What was unusual about that? Kaylin was six months old at the time and was being carried by her mother because she wasn't old enough to walk. Her mother, Jennifer Frederich, alerted the media, prompting a quick apology from Burger King.

Cold case. Many states restrict or ban the sale of cold medicines that contain the ingredient pseudoephedrine because it can be used to make crystal methamphetamine. In Indiana, you can buy only a certain amount of pseudoephedrine-based medicines in a seven-day period (and you have to fill out a form). But 70-year-old Sally Harpold didn't know that. One day in 2009, she bought a box of Zyrtec for her husband (who had allergies), and a few days later she bought her adult daughter some Mucinex-D for a cold. That put her over the purchasing limit, so Harpold was arrested for intent to manufacture crystal meth. The charges were later dropped.

He was unarmed. Steve Valdez of Tampa, Florida, went to a Bank of America branch in August 2009 to cash a check from his wife, but the bank refused to cash it. Why? Because B of A required a thumbprint as a form of identification, and Valdez could not provide one: He has two prosthetic arms. Even after presenting two forms of identification, he was denied and told by the manager to either come back with his wife or open an account. Bank of America later apologized to Valdez.

Alex remains silent. In 2007 Shelby Sendelbach, a sixth-grader at Mayde Creek Junior High in Katy, Texas, confessed to writing "I love Alex" on the wall of the school gym. Shelby was called to the principal's office, questioned by a police officer, read her rights, and charged with a "Level 4 infraction"—the same level applied to gun possession and making terrorist threats. (Only Level 5—for sexual assault and murder—is worse.) And she was sentenced to a special "disciplinary" school for four months. Officials said they were just following the rules. (They later reversed their decision and made Shelby write a letter of apology.)

Babyfat. In 2009 Colorado's Rocky Mountain Health Plans (RMHP) refused to cover Alex Lange because he had a preexisting condition: obesity. Alex's parents were furious. Why? "He's only four months old," his father, Bernie, said to reporters. "He's breast-feeding. We can't put him on the Atkins diet or on a treadmill." Amid all the negative press ("RMHP Denies Healthy but Big Baby!"), the company explained that it had a relatively new process of determining which babies were most "insurable"—and at 17 pounds, Alex didn't make that list. RMHP has since changed its policy to insure any healthy baby, regardless of weight.

Wackberry. In 2012 Chris Evans used his brand-new BlackBerry, which he hadn't quite figured out yet, to text a filthy come-on to his girlfriend. Except that he didn't send it to his girlfriend. Well, he did, but he also sent it to every single person on his contacts list. That alone would make for embarrassment several dozen times over, but it gets worse. Evans, 24, is a community-center swimming teacher in Birmingham, England.  The message was sent to two female students, 13 and 14 years old. Under British law, that's a sexual offense against a minor. Evans was sentenced to 18 months in prison but was released after two—the judge said Evans's mistake was due to "misguided use" of his BlackBerry.

IT'S THE COMPUTER'S FAULT

I n 2012 Microsoft debuted the Surface, a tablet computer designed to compete with Apple's iPad. The company spent $400 million to promote it, some of which went to secure a spot on Oprah Winfrey's annual "Favorite Things" list. (When she had a talk show, Winfrey held an annual "Favorite Things" episode in which she showered her studio audience with luxurious products, almost all of which were provided by their manufacturers for a fee. Winfrey does a special called *Oprah's Favorite Things* on the Oprah Winfrey Network now.) In November 2012, Winfrey wrote to her 14 million Twitter followers, "Gotta say love that SURFACE! Have bought 12 already for Christmas gifts." However, programs that deliver tweets also display how tweets are sent, such as a desktop computer, mobile phone, or, as in the case with Winfrey's tweet, an iPad.

• Shortly after the death of Apple's Steve Jobs in 2011, Margie Phelps of the Westboro Baptist Church announced plans to picket Jobs's funeral to protest America's tolerance toward homosexuality: "He had a huge platform; gave God no glory and taught sin." Phelps announced the picket via Twitter, from her Apple iPhone.

CRUSH CRASH

I n the 1890s, the Missouri-Kansas-Texas Railroad was having trouble attracting customers
in Texas, large parts of it dusty expanses, so
the company tasked executive William Crush with
boosting M-K-T business there. Crush's idea: a
massive publicity stunt in which the railroad would
build a small, temporary city where it would stage
a train crash. Back then, as now, people loved to
watch things crash into each other.

The railroad approved the plan. In 1896 it funded
the building of the town of Crush, Texas, 15 miles
north of Waco. The new little town consisted
mostly of tents and a large grandstand. In the
weeks leading up to the big event, two trains were
decorated and sent around Texas to lure people to
Crush—via the M-K-T Railroad at special reduced
rates, of course. By the date of the planned crash,
September 15, 1896, more than 40,000 people had
come to Crush, making it the second-largest city
in Texas (at least for the day).

A special track had been built 50 feet back from
the throngs, and police were on hand to hold back
the crowd. At 5:00 p.m., two trains were set to
full speed and aimed at each other. Then the crew
abandoned the 35-ton trains in preparation for impact. And, indeed, the trains did smash into each
other in spectacular fashion at 45 mph.

What Crush, M-K-T, and the crowd didn't expect, however, was the collateral damage. The force of the impact erupted the boilers on both trains, triggering massive explosions and hurtling debris into the crowd at high speeds. Photos of the event were taken by a man who was hit in the eye by a flying bolt, for example. Three spectators were instantly killed.

> **"WHAT CRUSH, M-K-T, AND THE CROWD DIDN'T EXPECT, HOWEVER, WAS THE COLLATERAL DAMAGE."**

The town of Crush was dismantled within a day; families of victims were given free tickets on the M-K-T Railroad. Crush himself was fired, then rehired by the railway when he convinced his bosses that he could spin the event into a public relations piece about proper railroad safety.

LAMBO, FIELD

In 2008 David Dopp won a brand-new $300,000 Lamborghini Murcielago LP640 in a Utah convenience-store sweepstakes. The first night he had the car, Dopp rounded a curve at 45 mph, hit a patch of black ice, then spun out. The car jumped a curb and crashed through a fence before stopping in a field about 75 feet from the road. The car was nearly totaled. Amount of time Dopp owned the intact Lamborghini: six hours.

UNINTENDED CONSEQUENCES

GOBBLED

In 1959 a program was started to aggressively introduce wild turkey populations to California. Officials hoped that having the game birds would mean big revenue from local and out-of-state hunters. It worked: By 1969 there were enough turkeys for a regular hunting season. By the 1980s, there were tens of thousands of them. And so, by 2003 California officials began introducing programs to get rid of wild turkeys, which now numbered in the 250,000 range. Biologists said they were invading habitats of native birds, consuming endangered plants and animals, damaging crops, ruining gardens, fouling backyards—and sometimes even attacking children.

SLIP, SLOP, SLAP, FLOP

After a hole was discovered in the ozone layer above Australia in the early 1980s, the Australian government launched aggressive ad campaigns to warn people about the risks of getting too much sun. (The ozone layer acts as a filter against the dangerous ultraviolet rays in sunlight, and the country already had the highest skin cancer rates in the world.) One of the most popular campaigns was "Slip, Slop, Slap": "Slip on a shirt, Slop on sunscreen, and Slap on a hat!" National health associations credited the campaign with making sunscreen use a normal part of life for many Australians, saving countless lives. Then, in 2000, officials announced that nearly 25 percent of Australian adults were deficient in vitamin D. How do you get vitamin D? Primarily by exposure to sunlight—the skin produces it in reaction to the sun's rays. Lack of the vitamin can cause a host of health risks, including osteoporosis, and is believed to be linked to breast, colon, and prostate cancer.

ORGAN FAILURE

Robin Cook's novel *Coma* was a pop-culture sensation in the late 1970s. It reached the *New York Times* bestseller list and was among 1977's top-selling thriller and fiction titles. In 1978 it was adapted into a hit movie (directed by another novelist, Michael Crichton). The plot: a major hospital deliberately puts surgery patients into comas so it can sell their organs for huge sums on a very active black market. The book's success was felt not only on the book and movie charts, but in real life as well: in the years after *Coma*, organ donation in the United States dropped by 60 percent.

> "IN THE YEARS AFTER *COMA*, ORGAN DONATION IN THE UNITED STATES DROPPED BY 60 PERCENT."

PIANO, MAN

For more than two years, John and Penny Adie, organizers of an annual classical-music festival in England, had been working tirelessly to raise enough money to buy a Bösendorfer grand piano for the festival. Valued at £45,000 ($89,000) and made exclusively in Austria, Bösendorfers are the preferred piano of many of the world's greatest players. "They're the Stradivarius of the piano world," said John.

By April 2007, they had finally raised all the money they needed, and they purchased the piano at a London auction. The only thing left to make their dream a reality was to deliver the Bösendorfer to the concert hall. As the delivery workers were hauling "the Stradivarius of the piano world" up the walkway, 20 feet from their destination, they lost control of the dolly...and John and Penny watched in horror as their prized piano fell eight feet off of a ledge and smashed discordantly onto the ground below. "It was a total loss," said John, noting that insurance would probably cover only half of what the piano was worth. "It's more than money that is the issue here," John said. "It was like seeing a priceless painting torn to shreds," Penny added.

PARLOR TRICKS GONE WRONG

Go diamondbacks! To show off to his friends in September 2007, a man in Portland, Oregon, put his pet eastern diamondback rattlesnake's head into his mouth... and it bit him. He barely survived. "It's actually kind of my own stupid fault," he said.

Just keep swimming. During a summer 2009 flood in Chattanooga, Tennessee, a 46-year-old man was standing near a raging culvert of water. Wearing only a pair of shorts, he bet his friends $5 that he could swim across the culvert. No one took the bet. He jumped in anyway. His body was found five days later, a mile and a half away.

Hand, gun. In 2009 a Falmouth, Massachusetts, man bragged to a friend that if the friend shot a BB gun at him from across the room he'd catch the pellet with his hand. The friend obliged. Good news: The man actually did snatch the BB out of the air with his hand. Bad news: The BB ended up lodged in his hand. He later explained to police at the hospital that the whole incident was just an "accident gone wrong."

THE $320,000 GOLF CLUB

It's never fun to give your boss bad news. And it's worse when the bad news is your own fault. Just ask Miles Byrne, who was caddy for golfer Ian Woosnam during the 2001 British Open. After three days of play, Woosnam was tied for the lead. On the final day, his first tee shot was just inches from being a hole-in-one. Standing on the second tee, Woosnam knew the biggest win of his career was in reach. Then Byrne gave him the news.

"There's too may clubs in the bag."

PGA rules are strict and clear: A golfer is allowed to have only 14 clubs, and Woosnam had an extra driver. The error cost Woosnam two strokes, raising his score on the first hole from a two to a four. Woosnam, an ex-boxer, yelled at Byrne, reportedly saying, "I gave you one job to do, and this is what happens," but then composed himself and finished the tournament tied for third place, winning around $300,000. Without the two-stroke penalty, he would have won $320,000 more and the title. Right after learning of the penalty, Woosnam threw the club, probably the most expensive in history, into the woods. Woosnam fired Byrne two weeks later.

TERRIBLE-BODY-ART-DECISION.COM

tatistics are unavailable for just how many people took part, but "skinvertising" was a widely reported element of dot-com boom in the 2000s. What was it? In those days of brash marketing and wild campaigns for name recognition by new web companies, startups would pay people anywhere from $1,000 to $10,000 to tattoo the company's name on their bodies. It was stunt marketing, the provenance of aggressive new companies at the frontier of the new web economy. And what happened to so many of those web companies? Many of them went out of business. But many of the tattoos live on.

- In 2003 Jim Nelson got a tattoo on the back of his head for CI Host.

- Mark Greenlaw still has a tattoo on his neck advertising web hosting company Glob@t (which is still around).

- Joe Tamargo is a walking billboard for 15 web companies, most of them now defunct, including PillDaddy.com (a Viagra marketer) and SaveMartha.com (a site aiming to get Martha Stewart out of prison, during her brief residency in the slammer).

- Karolyne Smith still has an ad on her forehead for GoldenPalace.com, an online casino. The site is still around, but most online gambling was outlawed in the U.S. in 2011, meaning the mother of four carries a facial ad for an illegal service.

- A man named Billy Gibby sold the rights to rename him to web hosting company Hostgator—his legal name is still Hostgator Dotcom. He has 37 tattoos, many on this face. He sold flesh ad space to GoldenPalace.com to pay for medical bills incurred after he gave his kidney to a friend in need.

MOVIE MISTAKES THAT WORKED OUT

The Usual Suspects (1995) is about five criminals who commit a robbery together after meeting at a police lineup. Near the beginning of the movie, in the lineup scene, each is supposed to step forward and repeat a line allegedly heard by a witness at a crime scene. For some reason, all five (played by Kevin Pollak, Stephen Baldwin, Gabriel Byrne, Kevin Spacey, and Benicio Del Toro) laugh to varying degrees as they say the line. The script called for the scene to be serious, so why the laughter? Del Toro was repeatedly farting during the scene, and his silent but powerfully stinky gassy bouts were making his co-stars crack up.

> **"HIS SILENT BUT POWERFULLY STINKY GASSY BOUTS WERE MAKING HIS CO-STARS CRACK UP."**

In **Zoolander (2001)**, former hand model and conspiracy theorist J.P. Prewitt (David Duchovny) explains to incredibly dumb male model Derek Zoolander (Ben Stiller) that all major historical assassinations have been planned by the fashion industry. Derek then asks, "But why male models?" and Prewitt explains in a lengthy monologue.

Then Derek responds, "Why male models?" again. He'd forgotten his original line and just repeated the other one instead. Stiller, the film's writer and director, kept the mistake in because it added to the characterization of Derek Zoolander as incredibly stupid.

A scene in *Being John Malkovich* (1999) has John Malkovich (played by John Malkovich, of course) angrily walking down the road. As scripted, a car full of extras was supposed to drive by. Instead, one of those extras leans out the window and shouts, "Hey Malkovich! Think fast!" and throws a can at Malkovich and hits him in the head. The actor gets noticeably mad. Director Spike Jonze thought it fit the scene—angry Malkovich—perfectly. The extra even got bonus pay.

One of the biggest themes of Woody Allen's *Annie Hall* (1977) is that his character, Alvy Singer, is a neurotic nerd, hopelessly outclassed by the cool, cosmopolitan Annie (Diane Keaton). In one scene, the couple go to a party and are handed a small container filled with cocaine. As Alvy takes the tin, he lets out an enormous sneeze, sending white powder everywhere. All the actors burst out laughing. As it made Alvy look about as nerdy as possible, Allen kept the sight gag in the movie.

BAD TRACTOR

Merle Watson was a folk singer and the son of folk-singing legend Doc Watson. Late one night in 1985, the younger Watson, 36, couldn't sleep, so he went to the basement of his Lenoir, North Carolina, farmhouse and started cutting some wood. But his saw got caught up in a knot, and a huge splinter shot up and pierced the muscle of his left arm.

No one else was there, and Watson couldn't remove the splinter. And he was bleeding. So he went outside and jumped on his tractor, hoping that one of his neighbors would still be awake. He saw a house on top of a nearby hill with the lights on, so he raced the tractor up there as fast as he could before he passed out. The nice couple brought Watson inside and removed the splinter. Then they bandaged up his arm.

He thanked them and set off for home. But he was tired and had lost a lot of blood. While trying to steer the tractor down the couple's steep drive-way, Watson hit the brakes and they locked up. The tractor skidded over an embankment, flipped over, and landed on top of Watson, crushing and killing him.

COWBOY UP!

The NFL's Dallas Cowboys are one of the most famous sports franchises in the world and, according to *Forbes*, the most valuable team in the NFL, worth $2.1 billion. The team's online home: dallascowboys.com. But in 2007, the even more streamlined "cowboys.com," purchased and locked down years before and left unused by a "squatter," became available. Website names of common words, such as "cowboys," do not come cheap, and yet it didn't seem odd to Dallas Cowboys management when they secured the rights to cowboys.com from a domain name agency for a measly $275.

"IT DIDN'T SEEM ODD TO DALLAS COWBOYS MANAGEMENT WHEN THEY SECURED THE RIGHTS TO COWBOYS.COM FROM A DOMAIN NAME AGENCY FOR A MEASLY $275."

They actually hadn't secured it at all. Because the price was actually $275,000, not $275. A front-office representative thought that the "275" mentioned in a phone conversation with the domain seller meant "275," while the seller meant "275,000." When the NFL team elected not to pay the very high fee (which it could easily afford), cowboys.com went up for sale at auction, where the Dallas Cowboys acquired it...for $375,000.

The Cowboys' communications team set up cowboys.com to redirect traffic to DallasCowboys.com, since that address was well established. But website owners must occasionally renew their domain name registrations. Cowboys.com was up for renewal in 2012, and the Dallas Cowboys let it expire. Result: cowboys.com became available for purchase again. Millionaire Match, which runs an array of dating and matchmaking websites, purchased cowboys.com...which is now a cowboy-themed gay dating website.

The Cowboys aren't the only NFL team without the rights to their own name online. The Chicago Bears, for example, can't get bears.com, because that's a place to buy teddy bear T-shirts.

BOXING DAY

In August 2012, Hu Seng of Chongqing, China, had a friend tape him shut inside a cardboard box, and then call a delivery service to be shipped to his girlfriend as a romantic surprise. The delivery was supposed to take 30 minutes, but the company went to the wrong address—and it took three hours to get to the girlfriend. When the girlfriend opened the box, she found her unconscious boyfriend inside. Seng and his friend had not thought to put any airholes in the box. (Surprise!) He was briefly hospitalized but made a full recovery.

MISSING THE (DECIMAL) POINT

In 1986 shipping company U.S. Lines was having trouble paying its debts. Especially worrisome was the $93 million it owed to Prudential Insurance. Held as collateral on the loan: U.S. Lines' fleet of cargo ships, which included some of the largest ships on earth. Prudential agreed to restructure the loan, but it wasn't until after U.S. Lines went bankrupt that anyone noticed a problem with the paperwork. The loan should have been $92,885,000, but someone had written it as only $92,885. Prudential lost over $90 million, including $11 million they had to give to U.S. Lines after selling off five of the cargo ships.

• In 2010 JP Morgan Chase offered currency trader Kai Herbert a job in South Africa. The job paid 2.4 million rand (about $320,000) per year, but things got even better for Herbert when someone flubbed his contract and wrote his salary as 24 million rand. Herbert signed the contract and hoped no one would notice. Chase caught the mistake before his first day. Herbert sued them for $1 million, a number that included compensation for "lost earnings." The judge disagreed, saying that Herbert's claim was "a gross exaggeration," and in the end, Herbert got nothing.

WEIRD WAYS TO DIE

Blowin' in the wind. A Nebraska woman was killed by Taco Bell. Not the food, but the sign. She parked her pickup truck in the restaurant's lot after arranging to meet someone who was going to buy her two dogs (which were in the back seat of the pickup). She said she'd be parked "under the Taco Bell sign." While she was waiting for the buyer, a strong gust of wind blew the sign over; it landed directly on the cab of the pickup, killing the woman. Her dogs were unharmed.

On a roll. In 1991 Edward Juchniewicz, 76, had a doctor's appointment in Canonsburg, Pennsylvania. An ambulance brought him from his nursing home to the appointment. But the paramedics left him in the parking lot on a gurney while they went inside to make sure the doc was ready. The unattended gurney started rolling away. It hit a curb, flipped over, and sent Juchniewicz onto the pavement. He died from severe head injuries.

Breathless. The problem with getting naked, putting a condom over your head, and then suffocating to death in bed is that when your body is found, the newspapers will all say you were found naked in bed with a condom over your head. That bizarre end came to Gary Ashbrook, who was also found with three empty nitrous oxide cartridges.

That sucks. On April 28, 1988, Clarabelle "C.B." Lansing was dutifully performing her routine as a flight attendant on Aloha Airlines Flight 243 when a small portion of the plane's bulkhead came off. One second, Lansing was standing in the aisle collecting empty drink cups; the next second, she got sucked out through the hole. Dozens more people were hurt, but the pilots were able to safely land the compromised aircraft. The only fatality was Lansing.

Just dessert. In 1995 an exotic dancer from Italy named Gina Lalapola was hired to jump out of a cake at a stag party. After climbing inside, the cake was sealed. But then it took an hour to get to the cake-jumping-out portion of the party. When Lalapola's cue arrived, she did not. The men waited. Still no stripper. So they opened up the cake and found her inside. She'd run out of air and died. Party over.

Woodn't you know?
Famed playwright Sherwood Anderson was eating appetizers and hors d'oeuvres on a cruise ship in 1941. He didn't take the toothpick out of one of those treats, swallowed it, developed peritonitis from it, and died.

THE DEAN OF ERRORS

In August 2006, legendary Australian cricket player Dean Jones was covering a tournament in Colombo, Sri Lanka, for Australian TV network Ten Sport when he said, "The terrorist has got another wicket." By "got another wicket," Jones was saying that someone had gotten a player out. By "terrorist," Jones was referring to South African player Hashim Amla, the first Muslim ever to play for the South African national team. Jones had thought he had said the remark quietly enough to not be picked up by the mic—but he was wrong. The public outcry was so immediate and so immense that Jones was on a plane out of Sri Lanka—and fired from his job with Ten Sport—within hours. Jones issued a contrite public apology, saying the comment had simply been a stupid attempt at humor.

A year later, Jones received a Father of the Year award from his Australian home state of Victoria. In 2010 that became another source of awkwardness when it was discovered that Jones, a married father of two, had been having an affair with a flight attendant for the previous nine years and had even had a child with her—a child he had never met. The state of Victoria took his Father of the Year Award back.

POORLY NAMED PRODUCTS

Vergatorio is a derivative of a Spanish slang term for the male genitalia. It's used throughout Latin America, except in Venezuela, where it means "reliable," which is why it's used as the name of a cell phone model issued by a state-run mobile phone company.

At one time, "gay" meant the same thing as "happy," whereas today its most prominent usage is as a synonym for "homosexual." Nevertheless, **Golden Gaytime** is a popular ice cream brand in Australia. Four-pack boxes promise "four delicious chances to have a gay time!"

Mitsubishi marketed its rugged, terrain-punishing Montero sport utility vehicle in Spain under the name **Pajero**. That word means "self-abusing" in Spanish, with Mitsubishi's marketing department thinking it implied a car that can take a beating from the elements. In Spain, the word's meaning is more akin to "self-pleasuring."

In 2011 Elmer's Glue debuted an all-in-one caulking gun and caulk: the **Squeez 'N' Caulk**.

The name of a plastic contraption that saves half-smoked cigarettes for later? The **Butt Buddy**.

The Nintendo DS is a handheld, touch-screen video game unit. In 2005 a Korean software company released an interactive DS dictionary program for kids called **Touch Dic**.

....

The Swedish furniture chain IKEA names most of its products after Swedish words. For example, the **FARTFULL** workbench.

....

If insects are a bother on your visit to Australia, just buy a bottle of **Wack Off!** repellent.

....

When a Nigerian state-run oil company started a joint venture with the Russian energy company Gazprom, they merged the words "Nigeria" with "Gazprom" and unfortunately got... **Nigaz.**

In the late 1970s, one of the leading diet products was a "reducing system" consisting of vitamins and an appetite suppressant candy. It's name: **AYDS.** (Once the AIDS health crisis hit, AYDS was done for.)

....

Like most grocery stores, Australia's Golden Circle chain has a line of store-brand products. One of those is a root beer-like, sarsaparilla beverage, which it calls **SARS.** That's also the name of a virus that killed nearly 800 people in a 2003 outbreak.

....

Belgian chocolatier Meurisse sells a nut-filled chocolate bar called **Big Nuts.**

....

JIMMY KIMMEL, FAR TOO LIVE

ABC got into the late-night comedy talk show game in February 2003. Competing with well-established comics Jay Leno on NBC and David Letterman on CBS, ABC offered Jimmy Kimmel, a radio veteran and host of *The Man Show* and *Win Ben Stein's Money* on Comedy Central. Producers planned a variety of ways to make *Jimmy Kimmel Live* different from the other guys, such as having a new guest co-host every week, airing the show live, and, to encourage a party atmosphere, serving alcohol to the studio audience, just as had been done on *The Man Show*.

Jimmy Kimmel Live debuted in the plum post–Super Bowl slot in January 2003. One woman in the audience apparently had a little bit too much to drink, because she threw up on her chair, just a few seats over from a network executive. After only one episode serving booze to the audience, ABC pulled *Jimmy Kimmel Live*'s liquor license. (Which is to say nothing of some other first-episode highlights, such as guest Snoop Dogg repeatedly flipping the bird to the camera, and guest George Clooney passing around a bottle of vodka onstage.)

THE HARTFORD COLISEUM COLLAPSE

I t had already been snow-ing for more than a week when the University of Con-necticut basketball team beat Massachusetts 56–49 at the Hartford Civic Center Coliseum on January 18, 1978. After the game, while 5,000 fans piled out into the snow, the colise-um's roof, a marvel of steel-truss engineering, was holding up 10 days' worth of accumulated snow and ice. Five hours later, it collapsed.

The roof, one of the first designed with com-puter-aided software, had a flaw. But it wasn't the computer's fault. The error came when the colise-um's architects had to transcribe the calculations into blueprints for the builders. At the time of the collapse, sections of the roof were overloaded by 852 percent. Amazingly, no one was hurt.

Rebuilding the coliseum—it reopened two years later and is now the XL Center—cost $75 million, not counting the millions lost by nearby busi-nesses who relied on revenue from basketball and hockey fans.

TO B-2, OR NOT TO B-2

I n February 2008, a ground crew was preparing a B-2 stealth bomber for takeoff at a U.S. Air Force base in Guam. They noticed odd readings coming from three sensors that relay information to the flight computer. Unfortunately, this particular crew hadn't heard about an "unofficial fix" for the problem: sending a blast of hot air through the system to evaporate any moisture on the sensors. Instead, they recalibrated the sensors and cleared the plane for takeoff. But as it sped down the runway, the moisture evaporated.

Result: The sensors sent incorrect data to the computer. "The pressure differences were miniscule," said Maj. Gen. Floyd Carpenter, "but they were enough to confuse the flight control system." As the plane lifted off, the pilots thought they were traveling at 158 knots but were actually only going about 124 knots.

The plane immediately stalled; the pilots ejected as the left wing dragged against the ground...right before the $1.2 billion bomber erupted in a huge fireball.

"THE PRESSURE DIFFERENCES WERE MINISCULE, BUT THEY WERE ENOUGH TO CONFUSE THE FLIGHT CONTROL SYSTEM.."

EXCERPTS FROM ACTUAL INSURANCE CLAIMS

• "I was driving along the motorway when the police pulled me over onto the hard shoulder. Unfortunately I was in the middle lane and there was another car in the way."

• "The accident happened because I had one eye on the lorry in front, one eye on the pedestrian, and the other on the car behind."

• "I pulled away from the side of the road, glanced at my mother-in-law, and headed over the embankment."

• "I saw a slow-moving, sad-faced old gentleman as he bounced off the roof of my car."

• "In an attempt to kill a fly, I drove into a telephone pole."

• "I was thrown from my car as it left the road. I was later found in a ditch by some stray cows."

• "Going to work this morning I drove out of my drive straight into a bus. The bus was five minutes early."

• "The accident was caused by me waving to the man I hit last week."

• "The guy was all over the road. I had to swerve a number of times before I hit him."

POLITICAL GAFFES

Darkest desert. In 2006 Amir Peretz was appointed defense minister of Israel, a controversial and unpopular choice, as Peretz didn't have a military background. Suspicions about his lack of expertise were confirmed decisively in February 2007. On a surveying trip with his chief of staff, the chief kept pointing out things for Peretz to look at. Photographers captured Peretz nodding as he acknowledged whatever he saw when he looked out of a pair of binoculars, which would have been hard, because the lens caps were still on.

Drawing a blank. During the 2005 election, leaders of the UK's Liberal Party sent out a letter to members of Parliament (MPs) in closely contested districts, playing up the achievements of the party's recent achievements. It was a form letter that MPs were supposed to personalize before sending out to their constituents. Instead, nine MP offices simply copied the letter whole and sent it out to thousands of homes, without inserting their town names, as per instructions. One excerpt: "And nowhere can we be more proud than here in."

Aye, Spy! *Spy* magazine decided to call out politicians on what it hypothesized was common: They have no idea what they're talking about and will tell reporters what they want to hear. A member of the *Spy* staff, impersonating a radio host, called members of the newly elected 1993 Congress. Among serious questions, they threw in, "Do you approve of what we're doing to stop the ethnic cleansing in Freedonia?" "It's very, very sad. We need to take action to assist the people."—Corrine Brown, Florida. "Anything we can do to use the good offices of the U.S. government to assist stopping the killing over there, we should do."—James Talent, Missouri. Jay Dickey of Arkansas blamed the newly elected President Clinton. Steve Buyer of Indiana said that "it's a different situation than the Middle East." Indeed, it is. Because Freedonia is a fictional country from the Marx Brothers movie *Duck Soup*. There is no such place.

Pay Moore attention. Tom Moore Jr. was working as a representative from Waco in the Texas Legislature in 1971 when he became worried that his fellow lawmakers didn't fully read or even pay any attention to the bills and resolutions they were tasked with passing. So Moore introduced a motion honoring Albert DeSalvo for his work in population control, praising his "dedication and devotion to achieve and maintain a new degree of concern for the future." The motion passed unanimously. DeSalvo, who is better known by his nickname the "Boston Strangler," murdered 13 women in Boston in the 1960s.

Free labor. Tommaso Coletti was president of Chieti, a province in southern Italy. In order to help promote employment assistance centers in the area in 2006, he approved an ad campaign with the slogan "Work makes you free." "I don't remember where I read this phrase but it was one of those quotes that have an instant impact on you because they tell an immense truth." It should have been familiar. It was the slogan the Nazis used at the concentration camps during in World War II.

Hardy, har-har. Benito Mussolini, dictator of Italy during World War II, was very short. Thinking that short stature equated with weakness, he used a variety of tactics to look taller, including standing on hidden stools during speeches and sitting in a special extra-high chair. When he first came to power, he also wore a bowler hat, until advisors told him the British news media said it made him look like "the fat one" from Laurel and Hardy.

You're doing it wrong. In 1983 China's health ministry conducted a massive population-control drive, as the country was rapidly outgrowing its resources (today China has more than a billion residents). TV ads, print ads, seminars, and home demonstrations were conducted to show people how to prevent the conception of children they didn't want. Birth-control pills and condoms were distributed by the millions. After one year, there was no decline. The reasons were revealed in a survey of participants: 80 percent of men had taken the birth-control pills, which were intended for women, and a whopping 98 percent of the men wore the condoms on a finger—because that's what the government instructors had done in their demonstrations.

"THE GOVERNMENT LOST MILLIONS ON UNUSED GAS."

The heat is on. The government of Bangladesh introduced a plan to defeat national poverty in 1982, helping its citizens financially by subsidizing heating gas, charging only a flat fee of $1.60 a month. Then the government found out that most people just left their ovens on all the time, since the gas was cheap, and they didn't have to buy matches to light the ovens. The government lost millions on unused gas.

Let's French! In 1890 the provincial government of Manitoba, Canada, passed a law declaring English to be the official language, contrary to Canada's federal English/French rule, because most Manitobans were English speakers. In 1985 the Canadian Supreme Court ruled that such a law was unconstitutional, because the Canadian constitution mandates bilingualism. That, in effect, rendered all laws passed in Manitoba since 1890 invalid. Lawmakers had to translate into French about 4,500 laws and 30,000 regulations, then reenact them all. It took five years.

GOOD ART, BAD BUSINESS

P*aradise Lost,* **lost.** Written in the 17th century, John Milton's *Paradise Lost* is one of the most important and widely read works in the history of the English language. Milton sold the rights to the first edition to a London bookstore for £10. After he died, his wife sold the rest of the rights for £8. Their financial loss? Immeasurable.

He didn't start the fire. It took English historian Thomas Carlyle most of 1834 to write the first volume of the three-part series *The French Revolution: A History*. Carlyle gave his only copy of the manuscript to a friend, economist John Stuart Mill, for critique. Mill never saw it—his maid thought it was wastepaper and used it to start a fire. Carlyle had to rewrite the entire book.

Starving artist. Italian painter Amedeo Modigliani, like many artists, was unrecognized for his talent during his life and, also like many artists, his work skyrocketed in value after his death in 1920. Modigliani had routinely traded his work for drinks and food, and when he died, café owners who had kept the paintings could cash in. Except for the café owner whose wife had scraped the paint off of their Modigliani so as to use the canvas to reupholster a sofa.

A CONVERSATION WITH "KEVIN SPACEY"

In 2007 actor John Cusack agreed to do an interview with *Take 5*, a pop-culture show on the University of Southern California's student-run television station. Minutes before the interview was to begin, the student host told Cusack she was missing her film class to interview him, adding, "It's so funny, because they're watching *American Beauty* today!" Puzzled, Cusack asked, "*American Beauty*? What's funny about that?" She answered, "You were in that!" For the record, Cusack was *not* in *American Beauty*. But Kevin Spacey, who, like Cusack, is a Caucasian, American, middle-aged film actor, *did* star in the film. But the student interviewer just kept pushing the issue. "*American Beauty*?" she said. Cusack said, "Nope." "What's the one with the rose petals?" she asked. "I'm not in that," Cusack responded. "That's not you?" she persisted. "No," said Cusack. "Really?" Cusack said, again, "No." She finally asked, "Am I just really confused?" To which Cusack responded, "I think you are."

The interview never aired. But the pre-interview described above ended up in a cringe-inducing video on YouTube, under the title "How NOT to start an interview." It has since been viewed millions of times.

LET'S PLAY HANGED-MAN!

"It's a fake noose, a prop noose!" insisted Joe McMahon, the owner of the Pink Punters nightclub in Buckinghamshire, England. The fake noose and gallows gets pulled out of storage every October for silly photo ops; it's low to the floor and "doesn't go tight 'round the neck." No one had ever managed to hurt themselves on it.

Until Richard Parry, a reveler wearing a Joker mask, put the noose around his neck during a 2012 Halloween party. He passed out with his neck in the noose, but it was impossible to know that because of the mask. Parry slumped over, his legs bent at the knees while his dangling, limp body swayed back and forth. His friends laughed and poked and prodded him while posing next to him for pictures. Finally, after about three minutes of dangling, a security guard noticed that something was wrong and rushed over and tried to get the Joker to respond. Parry just hung there, so the guard lifted him out of the noose. He wasn't breathing. The Halloween party came to an abrupt end as Parry was rushed to the hospital. After several scary hours, he finally came to and made a full recovery. McMahon is relieved Parry didn't die, but said he has no plans to get rid of the noose.

HOT MICS

MICROPHONE MALFUNCTION

During a 2009 concert in Tampa, Florida, Britney Spears finished a song, the arena went dark, and the crowd started cheering. Then, suddenly, the singer's voice could be heard over the speaker system, yelling, "My p**** is hanging out!" Spears had apparently had a wardrobe malfunction and was yelling to her stage techs, thinking her microphone was off. Videos of the incident were on YouTube within hours.

PUTTING THE "F" in "FCC"

In July 2008, veteran WNBC (New York) anchor Sue Simmons was getting ready to go to commercial when the video inexplicably went to a large ship in a harbor. After a second or so of silence, Simmons, still on a live mic, was heard by her millions of viewers saying, "What the f—?" The ship was on the screen for eight more seconds before the station cut to a commercial. When the news returned, Simmons apologized, saying she was "truly sorry" for using "a word that many people find offensive." What had happened—and who she was talking to—was never revealed.

AW, NUTS

In July 2008, Jesse Jackson was getting ready for an interview on Fox News when he leaned to the guest sitting next to him and, speaking about presidential candidate Barack Obama, whispered, "Barack's been talking down to black people. I wanna cut his nuts off!" Jackson wasn't on the air—but the remarks were caught on camera nonetheless, and someone got the tape to Fox News host Bill O'Reilly, who played it on his show. Jackson was forced to issue a hasty public response, especially since he publicly endorsed Obama's candidacy.

POTTY BREAK

Longtime CNBC host Bill Griffeth was interviewing former Treasury Secretary Larry Summers in April 2009 when the show was suddenly interrupted by the unmistakable (and very loud) sound of a toilet flushing. Griffeth paused, his head jerked to his left, his eyes narrowed, and, as the sound of the toilet receded, he said, "Anyway, we're going to take a quick break here..." and the show cut to commercial. A member of the technical staff had apparently forgotten to turn another guest's microphone off while they were doing their business. Griffeth didn't mention the gaffe when the show resumed.

WHY THE JUICE ISN'T LOOSE

In 1995 NFL Hall of Famer O. J. Simpson was found not guilty of murdering his ex-wife, Nicole Brown Simpson, and her friend Ronald Goldman. Simpson may have been acquitted, but the court of public opinion found him guilty. Simpson's career as an actor and pitchman (for Hertz and HoneyBaked Ham) was over. In a 1997 civil suit brought by Goldman's family, Simpson was found liable in the deaths and ordered to pay Goldman's family $33.5 million.

Initially, Simpson managed to avoid paying because California law protected his NFL pension. But the Goldmans didn't back down, and in 1999, Simpson auctioned off his Heisman Trophy and other memorabilia to pay the Goldmans $500,000. To avoid paying more (and to escape a $1-million-plus back-taxes bill), Simpson moved to Florida to protect his estate.

In December 2001, FBI agents searched his Florida home after receiving a tip that he was involved in a drug-trafficking ring. Authorities didn't find any narcotics on the premises, but they did discover that O.J. was pirating cable, leading to tens of thousands of dollars in fines and legal fees.

A year later, Simpson was caught speeding a 30-foot powerboat through a wildlife-protection zone and got hit with another fine. But despite his various run-ins with the law, he was still a free man.

Then, on the night of September 13, 2007, Simpson and a group of men burst into Bruce Fromong's room at the Palace Station Hotel and Casino in Las Vegas. Simpson was convinced that Fromong, a sports memorabilia dealer, had stolen some of his NFL mementos. Simpson and the group fled the scene after nabbing several items. The following day, he told a *Los Angeles Times* reporter that he wasn't a suspect. "I'm O. J. Simpson. How am I going to think that I'm going to rob somebody and get away with it?" He also contrarily quipped, "I thought what happens in Las Vegas stays in Las Vegas."

Unfortunately for Simpson, one of his accomplices brought a tape recorder along on the crime. The former NFL star was arrested a few days later on charges that included robbery and conspiracy. Simpson was found guilty on all charges and was sentenced to prison in December 2008. The presiding judge offered him little leniency and demanded that eight of the ten counts run concurrently for a maximum sentence of 33 years. Simpson is currently incarcerated in the Lovelock Correctional Center in Pershing County, Nevada, and is eligible for parole in 2017.

WHEN BOUNCY HOUSES GO BAD

In 2011 a bouncy house took flight during a youth soccer tournament on Long Island. A gust of wind caught the structure and carried it across a field, causing it to collide with two real houses and several bystanders. Parents rushed to the scene and frantically tried to grab hold of the flying house, to no avail. Thirteen people were injured by the time it finally came to a halt.

• A May 2011 fifth-grade graduation party in Tucson, Arizona, went horribly awry after a bouncy house got caught in a sudden gust of wind. The young grads inside all managed to escape before the house broke free and wrapped itself around a light pole. Six onlookers were hurt by flying debris.

• Also in Arizona in 2011, two 10-year-olds were seriously injured during a cultural festival when a freak dust storm blew a bouncy castle they were in 15 feet into the air, over a fence, and across a busy highway.

• A Pennsylvania man died in June of 2010 after sustaining injuries inside a bouncy house at a Cleveland Indians game. One of the inflatable sides collapsed, leaving him pinned underneath.

• In January 2011, winds carried another bouncy house away during a Florida birthday party. A five-year-old girl was caught inside. She was rescued by neighbors after the house landed in a pond.

• Inflatable houses and other attractions are still banned at many church festivals in southwest Ohio. The Archdiocese of Cincinnati issued a decree after an inflatable slide flipped over during a softball tournament in 2009. Wind threw the slide 70 yards and sent an 11-year-old boy along with it. Amazingly enough, he walked away from the accident with only a few bruises.

REAL 911 CALLS

A woman in Kissimmee, Florida, called 911 in April 2009 and said she was stuck in her car. "I cannot open my door. I can't get the windows down. Nothing electrical works," she told the dispatcher, adding, "and it's just getting very hot in here." The dispatcher asked the woman if she had tried to pull up the manual locks on the doors. The woman unlocked her door, got out, and apologized.

• In October 2011, a man in Hertfordshire, England, called 999 (the British equivalent of 911), and said, "There's something flying over our house. It's coming towards me now. I don't know what the hell it is!" The dispatcher spent several minutes taking the man's information, then told him she was contacting air authorities. The man called back a few minutes later, having figured out what the object was. "It's the moon," he said.

• Also in October 2011, a woman in Danvers, Massachusetts, called 911 to say that she, her husband, and her two children were lost. "I'm really scared," she said. "And we've got a baby with us," she added tearfully. The dispatcher tried to keep the woman calm, and a police K-9 unit rushed to the family's location—a Halloween maze cut into a cornfield. They were about 25 feet from the exit.

BLOCKBUSTED

In the early days of home video, up until the mid-1980s, video rental stores tended to be small operations, run locally, with a limited selection of titles. That changed with the arrival of Blockbuster Video, which opened its first four stores in the Dallas, Texas, area in 1985 and 1986. The difference: Blockbuster had a computerized checkout system and a whopping 8,000 titles in stock. The concept was clearly prime for success, and the small chain was sold to a group of investors with national chain experience. By the late 1990s, Blockbuster dominated the home video market, with more than 1,000 stores in the U.S.

By 2000 the company was already starting to lose value, but company leaders were offered the chance to purchase a new player on the movie rental scene: Netflix, which rented out DVDs via mail at a flat, monthly cost—with no late fees like the ones Blockbuster made millions from. (It's corporate legend, but Netflix founder Reed Hastings supposedly got the idea to start the company after returning *Apollo 13* to a Blockbuster six weeks late and paying a $40 late fee.)

Speculators saw great potential in Netflix. The young company was offered to Blockbuster for

$50 million—a price many analysts at the time called a bargain. But Blockbuster's corporate brass balked at the price and turned the deal down, instead spending millions in 2000 on a 20-year-deal to distribute movies digitally with a media subsidiary of the oil company Enron.

Yes, *that* Enron. The oil giant that went down in flames in a well-publicized accounting scandal about a year later, bringing down hordes of investors, executives, and deals along with it...including the one with Blockbuster.

Netflix, meanwhile, turned its first profit of $6.5 million in 2003 and was valued at about $4 billion in late 2012. But the choice to not purchase Netflix was just one bad decision in a series of missteps and bad luck for Blockbuster, including the launch of fresh competitors like the kiosk DVD rental company Redbox. Blockbuster tried an online subscription service, its own kiosk service, a "no-late-fee" policy (an advertising ploy that led to investigations for misrepresentation, resulting in the irony of a $650,000 fee for Blockbuster), and even a baffling bid to buy the struggling Circuit City. All these efforts failed to save the company. Plans to file Chapter 11 bankruptcy were announced in late 2010, and the remains of the company were purchased by Dish Network in 2011. Most stores were shuttered.

SORRY ABOUT THE RACISM

Can't be beat! Apple isn't the only company that makes personal digital music players. German company TrekStor entered the market in 2007, and, capitalizing on Apple's tendency to put "i" in the name of its products (iPhone, iPod, iPad, etc.), TrekStor called its device the i.Beat (as in beats, because it's a music player, get it?). However, the device was also colored black, leading TrekStor to release to the world a product called i.Beat.blaxx. Perhaps because of a language barrier, TrekStor was flummoxed by the outcry, and the company's president issued a press release stating that "beat" referred to music, not violence. Nevertheless, the company renamed the device the TrekStor blaxx.

Definitely unique. In 2012 Adidas announced plans for an athletic shoe that came with rubber shackles attached (shoe goes on the foot, shackle goes on the leg, for support or something). After many people on the Internet pointed out that foot shackles are primarily associated with slavery, and that basketball shoes have a large African-American customer base, Adidas pulled the shoe, but defended the design as "outrageous and unique."

McStupid. In 2002 a severe drought led to widespread famine in Africa—not the first time the continent had been ravaged by starvation. Somehow unaware of this, that same year McDonald's locations in Norway began selling a sandwich called the McAfrika, an "African-inspired" sandwich composed of pita bread, beef, and vegetables. After thousands of complaints and public shaming in the media, McDonald's pulled the sandwich and put famine relief donation boxes in its Norwegian outlets to help the estimated 12 million starving people in Africa at the time.

Bad Barbie. There have been hundreds of Barbie dolls released over the past several decades. In 1997 Barbie maker Mattel, in tandem with Nabisco, released an Oreo-branded Barbie to promote the popular cookie. The fact that Barbie's dimensions, if applied to a real woman, would negate the possibility of eating anything, let alone junk food, is not the most offensive aspect of this ill-advised marketing scheme. Mattel releases Caucasian and African-American versions of almost all of its Barbie dolls, and it did so with the Oreo-loving Barbie. Thus, a black "Oreo Barbie" made it to the market. Evidently neither corporation was familiar with the slang term "oreo," a derogatory term for a black person that means "black on the outside, white on the inside," like an Oreo, a way of calling a black person a sellout or accusing them of "acting white." (The doll was recalled.)

Sour milk. Dairy Queen introduced its version of the Starbucks Frappuccino in 2004. A combination of vanilla soft-serve ice cream and coffee, it was called the MooLatte, because it was a combination of dairy products (moo) and fancy coffee (latte). MooLatte, however, is very similar to the word mulatto, an outdated and offensive word that means "of mixed race." Dairy Queen apologized...but has kept the MooLatte on its menu to this day.

Not o-k-k-k. A 2011 alumni magazine for a University of Kentucky sorority ran a picture of three women in matching Kentucky tank tops, along with the caption "Sisters cheer for the Wildcats at a Kentucky football game." More than 200,000 readers saw the picture of three young, white women whose shirts spelled out "KKK."

The facts of "Life." Quaker's Life cereal comes in several varieties. The "regular" variety is packaged in a white box, and features a Caucasian woman and boy. Life's maple and brown sugar flavor comes in a brown box and shows two African American children.

Looney Zune. In 2006 Microsoft debuted the Zune, an MP3 player designed to compete with Apple's iPod. The name "Zune" was meant to sound like futuristic nonsense...until Hebrew scholars pointed out its similarity to the Hebrew *zi-yun*, which is basically that language's F-word.

HERE, I'LL SHOW YOU!

Clement Vallandigham was a 19th-century Ohio congressman and, during the Civil War, a leader of the little-known Copperheads faction: antiwar, pro-Confederate Democrats from the North. During the war, he was charged with treason, but President Lincoln commuted his two-year prison sentence to exile to the South. After the war, Vallandigham returned to Ohio and started a law practice. The night before a trial was to begin in 1871, Vallandigham was demonstrating to some of his law partners that his client, Thomas McGehan, was innocent of shooting Tom Myers to death, and that Myers had really shot himself.

So Vallandigham put a pistol in his pocket, pulled it out, cocked it...and shot himself, the same way he alleged that Myers had. McGehan was acquitted of murder, but he was represented by another lawyer, because Vallandigham had, evidently like Myers, accidentally shot and killed himself.

IT'S CRIMINAL

K **NOT FOOLED**
In 2003 a Pennsylvania family dressed their seven-year-old son in a Cub Scout uniform and sent him door-to-door to collect donations for his troop. Except that he wasn't really a Cub Scout—it was a scam, of course. They visited more than 150 homes and had earned $667 before they got caught. They knocked on the door of an Eagle Scout, who knew something was up when he saw a Cub Scout with a knotted kerchief. Cub Scouts use scarf slides, not knots.

FOOL ME ONCE...
In 1990 Charles J. Bazarian was convicted of swindling hundreds of thousands of dollars, which lead to the collapse of five savings-and-loan banks. He was prosecuted in Irvine, California. Three years later, as part of another swindling spree, Bazarian convinced the prosecutor who convicted him in 1990 to invest $6,000 in what turned out to be a fraudulent business.

CLICK? CLINK.
In 1993, 24-year-old David Bridges broke into a home in Grapevine, Texas, and stole a television. He probably would have gotten away with it, too, had he not returned to the home, where police were waiting, to retrieve the TV's remote control.

CUSTOMER SERVICE

Most bank robbers disguise themselves before they commit the crime. Others simply go to a place where they wouldn't be recognized. And then there's  the woman who in October 2012 went on a string of bank robberies in the Boston area. One of the banks she hit was the bank where she has an account. The teller she held up recognized her, called her by name, and easily led the cops to her home.

BLUFF CALLED

Derrick Johnson annoyed a Kansas City gas station clerk over the course of three months in 1990, coming in every few days and stealing food from a cooler, each time taunting the clerk by saying "Catch me if you think you can!" The last time, the clerk shot and killed him.

CARPET BAGGERS

In 1981 Dora Wilson of Harlow, England, looked out the window and saw some men moving her next-door-neighbor's prized collection of Persian rugs into a van. Wilson asked the men what they were up to, as the neighbors were away on vacation. The men replied that they were rug cleaners. Pleased at the opportunity, Wilson asked the crew if they would take her Persian rugs to be cleaned as well. They did, and neither Wilson nor the neighbors saw the rugs again. Obviously, the men were not rug cleaners.

BAD .COM NAMES

Who Represents is a resource for finding out what talent agent represents any celebrity:
Whorepresents.com.

Pen Island sells...pens at:
Penisland.com

Therapist Finder locates a therapist in your area:
Therapistfinder.com

Speed of Art is a design firm, not a swimsuit flatulence company:
Speedofart.com

Regency Technologies disposes of old computer or "IT" equipment, including running an IT scrap service, which explains the URL:
Itscrap.com.

Benjamin Dover is a financial planner and author:
Bendover.com

For information on New York State's many canals:
Nycanal.com

Dave Robins is a tree surgeon, or arborist, in France. He named his business from the French word for forests, *les bocages*:
Lesbocages.com

Although Americans are tough, they're not *that* tough; this site represents a scrap metal dealer:
Americanscrapmetal.com

Dickson makes data-entry and data-crunching software, and they probably get a lot more web traffic than they expect at:
dicksonweb.com

For a quick-reference guide on the expert web sites for information in insurance, travel, and Internet services (and that's it):
expertsexchange.com

When visiting the Hocking Hills region of Ohio, book lodging through Old Man's Haven Cabin Rentals:
Oldmanshaven.com

WHEN BEER ATTACKS

October 17, 1814, began like any other dismal London day, but it was about to get more dismal than usual. Several giant wooden vats of aged stout stood inside the Horse Shoe Brewery, a massive building that rose above the squalid slums of the St. Giles parish in central London. At half past four that afternoon, a brewery worker noticed that an 800-pound metal hoop had slipped off the lower section of one of the vats. He left a note for his supervisor about it and got back to work. About an hour later, workers heard a very loud, creaking noise coming from that vat.

And then all ale broke loose. More than 3,500 barrels' worth of 10-month-old porter erupted from the compromised vat. A 15-foot-high wall of a dark, full-bodied ale with a slight hint of mahogany took out more tanks. Then the torrent of beer crashed through the brewery's outer wall.

With no warning, a tsunami of stout, wood, and metal laid waste to several homes and businesses near the brewery. One unfortunate servant at the Tavistock Arms Pub was crushed when a wall collapsed on him. Seven women and children were killed in their homes. According to local legend, another man died a few days later of alcohol poisoning.

BAD LIBATIONS

BUM RUM

BUM RUM
A bar owner in Nicaragua brewed a small batch of rum and put it in cans. Bad idea: The cans once contained insecticide, and he hadn't washed them out very well. Eleven people were poisoned by drinking the tainted rum. When he was tried for 11 counts of poisoning, the barkeep tried to prove his innocence by proudly drinking a large glass of the rum. He died a few minutes later.

MAGNUM, P.O.

In 1989 New York wine merchant William Sokolin attended a ritzy $250-a-plate Bordeaux dinner for wine enthusiasts at New York's famed Four Seasons restaurant. He announced to the nearly 200 guests that he had acquired a bottle of 1787 Chateau Margaux, which Sokolin estimated to be worth around $520,000. And then it was worth nothing when he bumped it against a piece of furniture, poking two holes in the very old and very fragile bottle, from which most of the wine immediately leaked out.

STUMPED

Aman without an arm walked into a Bellingham, Washington, urology clinic in October 2011. "I hope that's a Halloween costume," said one of the urology techs. But the bloody stump was real. The armless man—whose name wasn't released, so we'll call him Stumpy—refused to cooperate with the urology techs, but they'd seen him before and assumed (correctly) that he lived in the woods near the urology clinic. Once Stumpy calmed down, he was transferred to a nearby hospital.

Police later found his campsite, his severed limb, and the device that had severed it: a 16-foot-tall guillotine. Stumpy had constructed it himself "in the medieval style." (No word on what he planned to use it for.) The arm was raced to the hospital, but doctors were unable to put Stumpy back together again.

> "POLICE LATER FOUND HIS CAMPSITE, HIS SEVERED LIMB, AND THE DEVICE THAT HAD SEVERED IT: A 16-FOOT-TALL GUILLOTINE."

A SHORT INTERVIEW

In May 2012, actor Martin Short appeared on *The Today Show* to promote his movie *Madagascar 3: Europe's Most Wanted*. Hosts Kathie Lee Gifford and Hoda Kotb asked Short a few questions about his kids, then Gifford started praising Short's wife. "He and Nancy have got one of the greatest marriages of anybody in show business," she said. "How many years on for you guys?" Short answered, "We, umm, married 36 years." Gifford leaned in and said, emphatically, "But you're still like in love." Short paused for a second, then answered, "Madly in love. Madly in love." Gifford asked, "Why?" Short answered, "Cute. I'm cute," to laughs, and the interview was soon over.

However: Short's wife, actress Nancy Dolman, had died of ovarian cancer in 2010. Short left the *Today* set without saying anything about what had happened, but a producer told Gifford what she had done, and she made an apology on the air immediately. After the show, Gifford tweeted, "I send my sincerest apologies to @MartinShort and his family. He handled situation w/enormous grace and kindness and I'm so grateful." Bonus gaffe: "@MartinShort" is not Short's Twitter handle. (It's "@MartinShortSays.") But Short did accept Gifford's apology, telling E! News, "It's live television and people make mistakes."

BASEBALL ERRORS

TRIPLE DIP

In the fourth inning of a game between the New York Yankees and the Milwaukee Brewers on July 27, 1988, the Brewers' Jim Gantner was on first base when Jeffrey Leonard hit a light tapper to the first-base side of the pitching mound. Yankees pitcher Tommy John tried to field the ball with his bare hand...and flubbed it. (Error.) He got control of the ball and threw it to first...over the head of first baseman Don Mattingly and down the right-field line. (Error.) Right fielder Dave Winfield got the ball and threw it toward home in an attempt to get Gantner out. John cut off the throw and threw it home...over the head of catcher Don Slaught. (Error.) John tied a record for pitchers, making three errors in one inning—but he'd done it on one play. "I think there were too many negative ions in the air," John said after the game.

HANKS A LOT

The 1924 World Series went about as far as it could go: a decisive game seven and into 12 innings. The score was tied at three when the Washington Senators' Muddy Ruel hit an easily catchable pop-up fly into foul territory behind home plate. It should have been an easy out for

New York Giants catcher Hank Gowdy, but some-how, someway, Gowdy got his foot caught in his catcher's mask. Instead of snagging the ball, he tripped over and fell down. Ruel, still at bat, then hit a double, and then scored the run that enabled Washington to win the World Series.

OFF THE DOME

On May 26, 1993, the Cleveland Indians were play-ing the Texas Rangers when Indian Carlos Martínez hit a long fly ball to right field. The Rangers' José Canseco ran back after it, looked as if he was about to catch it, lost sight of it...and then the ball hit him right on top of the head and bounced over the wall. Home run.

ITCHING TO PITCH

Three days after Canseco's gaffe, the Rangers were down 12–0 to Cleveland in the eighth inning. Since the game seemed unwinnable, Canseco asked his manager, Kevin Kennedy, if he could pitch—something he hadn't done since high school. Kennedy let Canseco take the mound. Not only did Canseco pitch badly—he surrendered three walks, allowed two hits, and three runs—he also injured his arm. Canseco had only a few at-bats in the next several games, and six weeks later finally had to have reconstructive surgery—and was out for the rest of the 1993 season.

LESS THAN PERFECT

On June 2, 2010, Detroit Tigers pitcher Armando Galarraga was about to complete a perfect game—pitching all nine innings and allowing no hits, walks, or runs. At the time, it had only been accomplished 20 times in Major League Baseball history. Galarraga had one ball and two strikes on the Cleveland Indians' Jason Donald. Galarraga threw, and Donald hit a soft grounder between first and second base. First baseman Miguel Cabrera ran to his right to get it as Galarraga streaked toward first. Cabrera snagged the grounder and tossed it to Galarraga, who caught it and tagged first at virtually the same time Donald got there. Umpire Jim Joyce called Donald safe. The crowd, the announcers, the players—most especially Galarraga—were stunned into silence. Donald, who had just been called safe, cringed and put his hands on his helmet—because even he knew he was out, and that Galarraga had been robbed of a perfect game. Footage of the incident—which was replayed thousands of times on sports shows all over the country in the following days—showed clearly that Donald was out. Galarraga got the next batter out, and the game ended—just another game. Umpire Joyce, a 23-year veteran and considered one of the best umps in the game, met with Galarraga and the press after the game and admitted that he'd gotten the call wrong. "I just cost the kid a perfect game," he said, tearfully apologizing to the Tigers pitcher. Galarraga quipped to reporters, "Nobody's perfect."

PLEASE HANG UP AND TRY AGAIN

AT&T used to invite customers to "reach out and touch someone," but for much of January 15, 1990, the only thing AT&T users could reach out to was a dial tone. At the time, AT&T handled 115 million calls a day, routing them through a nationwide network of switching stations. Around 2:00 p.m,. a station in New York went offline for a routine four-second diagnostic. Back online, an engineer informed the other stations it would start delivering calls again, which it did, 10 milliseconds later.

The close timing of the two messages confused a second switching station, causing it to reset. During the reset, a backup switch received two more closely timed messages, which caused it to reroute its calls. Which caused a *third* switching station to go offline, which shut down a fourth, and so on, until all 114 switching stations were down in less than three seconds.

At first AT&T thought they'd been hacked. The real problem: The switches had done exactly what they were programmed to do. When the company updated the computer system a year earlier, a programmer flubbed a line of code that would have kept the switches from resetting. It took AT&T nine hours to get the network back online. Between 50 and 70 million calls had been were lost.

STAGED DEATHS

Floored. In 1870 the James Robinson & Co. Circus and Animal Show wanted to drum up some publicity for its touring cavalcade  prior to a performance in Middletown, Missouri. As the clowns, circus performers, and animals paraded through town, the circus band was ordered to play while standing on the roof of a cage that held two lions. Despite concerns that the roof wasn't strong enough, circus managers forced the band to play on, and they did, up until the moment the roof caved in, plunging the musicians into the den of hungry lions, who tore them limb from limb and ate most of their bodies. Ten band members started the parade; only three survived the mauling.

No Tell-ing. Annie von Behren starred in an 1882 production of the play *Si Slocum*. One scene called for the actor playing opposite her, her real-life fiancé, Frank Frayne, to shoot an apple off of her head with a rifle—with his back to her. More than 2,300 people watched one night as Frayne pulled the trigger, releasing a bullet that missed the apple entirely in favor of von Behren's forehead.

PRESIDENT LANDON

The *Literary Digest* was among America's most popular and credible news and opinion magazines in the 1920s and '30s. More than a million Americans got their news, news analysis, and editorial opinions from *TLD* by 1927.

One of the magazine's most popular features was an exhaustive presidential straw poll in which it asked around 10 million Americans who they planned to vote for. It accurately predicted the winner of every presidential election from 1920 to 1932. *TLD* conducted the poll once more in 1936, declaring that the Republican challenger, Kansas governor Alf Landon, would defeat incumbent Democratic president Franklin Roosevelt, 57 to 42 percent, and with 370 electoral votes, a massive landslide for Landon.

Actual result of the 1936 presidential election: Roosevelt beat Landon 60.8 percent to 36.5 percent, and carried 46 of 48 states for an electoral college total of 523–8, the biggest landslide in history to that point.

How did *TLD* get it so very wrong? The people they polled did not represent a cross-section of the American electorate. In 1936 America was deep into the Great Depression. People struggled to feed and clothe themselves, and one of the casualties was magazines. Only the wealthy could afford a subscription to a magazine such as *The Literary Digest. TLD* included its own readers in its poll, but the bulk of survey respondents came from two other groups: owners of cars and telephones, both of which were exorbitantly expensive and also available only to the wealthy, and heavily Landon-favoring, voters of 1936.

The poll cast so much doubt on *The Literary Digest*'s credibility that it directly led to the magazine's end. Less than two years later, it was bought out by a competitor, *Review of Reviews*. That magazine went out of print less than a year later.

SILENCED *MARINER*

NASA's first mission to study the inner solar system was the Mariner Program, 10 unmanned space probes that visited Mercury, Venus, and Mars. *Mariner 1*, launched on July 22, 1962, was supposed to be a three-and-a-half-month flyby of Venus to gather information about its atmosphere.

Just after liftoff, the rocket carrying *Mariner 1* veered off course when a computer misunderstood the rocket's trajectory. A ground-based radar system had failed to account for the "radio echo," the time it takes a signal to reach its target and return to the ground. That 43-millisecond miscalculation meant that instead of going toward Venus, *Mariner* boomeranged back to Earth.

Fearing the rocket might crash into a populated area, mission control sent a self-destruct command to the probe. Less than five minutes after liftoff, *Mariner 1* exploded over the Atlantic Ocean. The mistaken course correction came from a line of code transcribed by a programmer working from a handwritten formula. Several theories exist about the specific mistake, but NASA's explanation is that the programmer missed a single hyphen. That hyphen cost $18.5 million.

THREE SPORTS GAFFES

FETCH!
Fewer than 300 pitchers have ever struck out more than 1,000 batters in the entire history of professional baseball. Atlanta Braves pitcher Charlie Leibrandt made it to that number in 1992. After he struck out his 1,000th batter in a game against the San Francisco Giants, the catcher paused the game and handed Leibrandt the milestone ball, which he threw into the Braves dugout for safekeeping. The problem: neither the catcher nor Leibrandt had called time-out or asked for a new ball, meaning the ball he'd thrown into the dugout was still technically in play. The runner on first realized it at about the same time as Leibrandt, so while he hustled to the dugout to retrieve the ball, the runner stole second base.

THE SLOW STEAL
The 1926 World Series came down to a decisive seventh game between the New York Yankees and the St. Louis Cardinals. The Yankees came up to bat in the ninth inning, with the Cardinals up 3–2, and two outs. With a full count, Babe Ruth earned a walk—the tying run. Power hitter Bob Meusel came up to bat, and if he got a hit, Ruth would score. Instead, Ruth, well known for being heavy-set and slow, and successful at base stealing only 50 percent of the time, decided to steal second

base on the first pitch. Cardinals catcher Bob O'Farrell easily threw him out. Game over, series over, Cardinals win.

BUT WHO'S COUNTING?

The University of North Carolina was heavily favored to win the 1993 NCAA college basketball tournament, but the big story was the University of Michigan's "Fab Five" lineup of freshmen and sophomore starters who had made it all the way to the final. Among the five were future NBA superstars Jalen Rose, Juwan Howard, and Chris Webber, an All-American that year. In the final game, North Carolina led 73–71 with just 19 seconds left. North Carolina's Pat Sullivan missed a free throw, and Webber quickly rebounded it and began to take it up the court.

Just past midcourt (and after traveling, which wasn't called), Webber called time-out, allowing Michigan to reset the clock and inbound closer to their net, and hope to turn at least a two-point play. The big problem with that common late-game strategy was that Michigan didn't have any time-outs left. Webber was called for a technical foul, and North Carolina got the ball back, sunk two free throws, and won the game.

MARRIAGE ACCIDENTS

HUSBAND-DAD

A 60-year old Ohio widow named Valerie Spruill learned a chilling truth in 2004: Her dead husband was actually her father! Sometime earlier she had found out that a "family friend" she grew up with was actually a prostitute...and her mother. Apparently, her father was only 15 years old when he knocked up a "woman of the night," and the little baby—Valerie—lived a very full life before finding the awful truth. When Spruill's story made national news in 2012, she served as a warning that familiar familial relations are not always what they seem to be.

HUSBAND-BROTHER

A South African couple had the picture-perfect relationship. After falling in love at first sight when they met at college in 2006, the lovebirds dated for five years. Then they became engaged. Then they finally got around to meeting each other's single parents. To everyone's surprise, the parents already knew each other. They'd been together in the 1980s and had two kids. After splitting up (mom cheated on dad), the sibling toddlers were separated and raised 50 miles apart. Making matters even more complicated: The sibling-bride-to-be was eight months pregnant. "I can't think straight right now," the horrified grandma-to-be told reporters. At last report, the sibling couple had split up.

HUSBAND-WIFE

Six months after she got married, Minati Khatua of Rourkela, India, discovered that her husband was actually a woman. She had suspicions that something was wrong because her "husband" would never let her see "him" naked. Khatua finally found out the truth by bursting into the bathroom one day when "he" was taking a bath: The husband had no...husband parts. S/he ran away, taking Khatua's Jeep and dowry money. S/he remains at large.

TWO ACCIDENTAL DEATHS

• Nancy Lincoln, mother of nine-year-old Abraham Lincoln, died in 1818 after drinking a glass of milk from the family cow, which had been grazing on poisonous snakeroot and passed the poison into the milk.

• A woman from Donetsk, Ukraine, thought she was opening a can of beer she found in a train station, but she was actually pulling the pin out of a grenade. (You know how that goes.) The woman died; 17 other people were injured.

DUH.COM

Furniture.com (1998–2000)

Great Idea: Save shoppers the hassle of going to a furniture store, picking out a table, and figuring out how to get it home.

Fatal Flaw: Only after the site's owners shelled out a whopping $2.5 million for the domain name did they discover that neither FedEx nor UPS would ship a couch. More-expensive shipping companies were required, which meant that a $200 table cost $300 to ship. Plus, items took an average of one month to arrive at the customer's home. The company lasted two years, falling apart in 2000. (The site is still live, albeit managed by a different company.)

Kozmo.com (1998–2001)

Great Idea: Deliver anything to anyone at any time.

Fatal Flaw: It cost more to get the products to the customers than the customers had to pay for them. Available in nine U.S. cities, Kozmo offered free delivery of "videos, games, DVDs, music, mags, books, food, basics & more" in less than one hour, with no minimum purchase. That meant that if a stoner wanted a bag of Doritos at 4:00 a.m., a Kozmo driver would have to track down the Doritos and make it to the stoner's apartment in lightning speed. Despite obtaining $280 million from investors, Kozmo never made a profit. By the time it went bankrupt, it was nearly $20 million in the hole, and its failure put 1,100 people out of work.

Flooz.com (1998–2001)

Great Idea: Start a new form of Internet currency and hire Whoopi Goldberg as spokesperson. With an A-list celebrity endorser on hand, Flooz founder Robert Levitan was able to wrangle $35 million from investors and line up 30 "e-tailers," including Barnes & Noble and Tower Records. Shoppers could earn "Flooz credits" (like airline miles) and then use the Flooz to buy real stuff at participating merchants.

Fatal Flaw: There already was a form of Internet currency...called "money." Traded in the form of "credit," this money was backed by federal agencies and large private banks. Flooz, as far as customers were concerned, was backed by Whoopi Goldberg. (And much of the investment money Levitan generated was used to pay her.) As online shopping became safer in 2000 thanks to encryption software and firewalls, online shoppers preferred to buy directly from the store rather than through a third party. When the company went bankrupt, all existing Flooz credits were nullified and non-refundable. "I am going to cry," grumbled one former Flooz holder. "I lost about $350. I have a good mind to write to Whoopi Goldberg!"

ON THE JOB

In May 2008, Charles Habib, a laborer with John Roth Paving Pavemasters in New Castle, Pennsylvania, was awaiting a delivery of asphalt with his coworkers when someone found a bowling ball near the parking lot they were repaving. The men had shot-putting contests with the ball for a while, then someone put up a challenge to see if one of them could break the bowling ball with a sledgehammer. Habib grabbed a sledgehammer and cracked the ball with the first blow. The crew foreman spoke up at this point, telling Habib to knock it off, and that he wouldn't be taking him to the hospital if he was injured. Habib smashed the ball again anyway, and a piece of the ball broke off—and flew straight into his right eye, cutting the eyeball. He required immediate surgery (no word on whether or not the foreman drove him to the hospital), and, worst of all: Habib eventually lost all sight in the eye. (Habib also lost his bid to get workers' compensation for the on-the-job bowling ball–smashing injury.)

When real estate agent Peter Collard arrived at the six-bedroom house he was trying to sell in Brisbane, Australia, in 2010, he was horrified to discover that half of the yard was dug up and 10 palm trees had been ripped out of the ground. Next to the devastation were two confused-looking workmen and a backhoe. When Collard asked them what they doing, the men quickly loaded the backhoe onto the trailer and, without a word, drove away. According to police, they were digging a swimming pool, but due to an address mix-up, they were at the wrong house. Collard's insurance company denied his claim for compensation. Cost of the repair: $20,000.

The Pilgrim Nuclear Power Plant was shut down for about a week in 1986. Reason: Some of the plant's employees were messing around and accidentally threw a rolled-up pair of gloves—a makeshift ball—into a backup safety tank.

On September 18, 1977, the Tennessee Valley Authority had to close its Knoxville nuclear power plant. The plant stayed shut for 17 days, at a cost of $2.8 million. Cause of the shutdown: "human error." A shoe had fallen into an atomic reactor.

In September 1978, a sailor accidentally dropped a 75-cent paint scraper into the torpedo launcher of the nuclear sub USS *Swordfish*. The sub was forced to scrap its mission so repairs could be performed in dry dock. Cost to U.S. taxpayers: $171,000.

THE JOHNSTOWN FLOOD

Lake Conemaugh, contained behind the South Fork Dam outside of Pittsburgh, was the private playground of the South Fork Fishing and Hunting Club, organized in the 1870s by steel tycoon Henry Clay Frick as a retreat for the city's upper crust. The club made several changes over the next decade that weakened the dam, including a wider roadway across the top to accommodate their luxury carriages. This lowered the dam, bringing it only four feet above the spillway that kept it from overflowing.

Heavy rains in May 1889 raised the lake to within a few feet of the roadway. By the morning of May 31, water was pouring over the top. Despite the club's last-minute attempts to reinforce it, at 3:10 p.m. the dam gave way, sending a 35-foot wall of water and trees—not to mention the remains of the dam—gushing toward Johnstown, 14 miles downstream. Survivors said the sound was "a roar like thunder."

Ten minutes after the water reached Johnstown, four square miles of the city were gone. Sixteen hundred homes were leveled. An official telegraphed Pittsburgh, saying simply, "Johnstown is annihilated." All told, 2,209 people died.

PROFESSOR RALPH

A Texas high school science teacher named Brandi Bastas nearly killed herself and her students in September 2012. She was showing the class how to identify certain proteins and amino acids. But she failed to demonstrate how to keep two volatile substances—nitric acid and cyanide—from combining. A little spill from a test tube onto the lab table was all it took.

Bastas told everyone to get away from the table. Then she ran into the hallway and started vomiting. Then one of her students felt a burning rash on his skin. Then another one did, too. Then more had trouble breathing. Describing the scene, student Karin Ortiz said everyone was "freaked out."

When the teacher and five affected students arrived at the nurse's office, school administrators thought it might be a good idea to evacuate the classroom and the adjacent rooms. Thankfully, the chemicals dissipated before any serious injuries occurred, but the victims had to be treated at a local hospital.

"BUT SHE FAILED TO DEMONSTRATE HOW TO KEEP TWO VOLATILE SUBSTANCES—NITRIC ACID AND CYANIDE—FROM COMBINING."

BAD TRIP

"AGAIN, AS THEY COULDN'T READ FRENCH, THEY STAYED ON THE TRAIN TOO LONG AND ENDED UP IN LUXEMBOURG, NOT PARIS."

The major cities of Europe are not all that far apart geographically, especially since a rail system unites the Continent. In May 1981, the Elthams, a couple from Dover, England, decided to take a day trip to Boulogne, in northern France, a distance of about 70 miles. They had a nice time sightseeing and shopping, but because they were unable to read French, they misread street signs and ended up wandering away from the town center and getting lost. Fortunately, they were able to explain the situation to some strangers, who gave them a ride back to the Boulogne train station, where they decided to take a train to Paris. The ticket took up most of the cash they had left.

Again, as they couldn't read French, they stayed on the train too long and ended up in Luxembourg, not Paris. Having been awake for over 24 hours during their odyssey, they fell asleep on the train ride back to Paris...and woke up in Basel, Switzerland. Swiss police sent them back to Belfort, France, where they were told that in order to make the Boulogne connection, they'd have to get to Montbeliard. Short on funds, they walked…15 miles. The town housed them for free in a hostel and allowed them to call home to Dover, but they couldn't reach any family or friends.

The Elthams then decided to get temp jobs in Montbeliard to earn money to get back to Dover, but again, they couldn't speak French, and there were no jobs to be had anyway. After a couple of days, the police escorted them back to Belfort. Once again, the Elthams wandered off and ended up walking 38 miles to Vesoul, from which they took a train into Paris. At the Paris train station, they read the schedules wrong and hopped a train to Bonn, Germany, where German police dumped them out just over the border, in Switzerland.

There, their luck changed. A policeman drove them to Boulogne, where they spent 24 hours in a holding cell explaining their ordeal to customs and immigration officials, who carefully put them on a train back to Dover. Or at least, to just outside of Dover. They walked the final 23 miles home.

4 REAL, UNFORTUNATELY NAMED BOOKS

Scouting for Boys

Pooh Gets Stuck

The Best Dad Is a Good Lover

Touched: The Jerry Sandusky Story

PERHAPS I MISSPOKE

Your pick! A Saskatoon, Saskatchewan, news anchor was talking up a local event in February 2012. She meant to tell viewers that they could get tickets online at Picatic.com. Instead, she said "pick-a-dick.com." She and her fellow female anchor immediately covered their mouths with their hands, then started giggling uncontrollably. The first anchor finally got herself together and repeated the new copy...and made the same mistake again. Bonus: The local event she was talking about was "King of the Kielbasa"—a sausage-making festival. And after she said "pick a dick" the first time, her co-anchor said, "Well, you were thinking about sausage."

J-Lo-no-no. During a November 2002 episode of his nightly Fox News show, Shepard Smith introduced a segment on singer Jennifer Lopez's new song, "Jenny from the Block," which he said was about how Lopez claimed to be just a humble girl from the Bronx. "But folks from that street," Smith continued, "sound more likely to give her a curb job than a blow ***." He then quickly blurted, "Block party!" and tried to continue the newscast, then after just a few seconds gave up. "I'm sorry about that," Smith said, looking pale. "I have no idea how that happened." Smith later said he "felt the blood go to my toes" when the words left his mouth. He also said, "I had to call my mother and apologize."

Holly terror. In June 2011, Roanoke, Virginia, news anchor Holly Pietrzak looked into the camera and told her viewers, live, on the air, "More teens are having f—." A look of horror then took hold of Pietrzak's face, after which she stammered, "ha-ha-having *luck*." She had meant to say, "More teens are having luck finding summer jobs." Pietrzak apologized at the end of the program, and WDBJ station manager Jeff Marks told reporters that Pietrzak would not be fired, saying what had happened was an honest mistake, adding, "Life goes on."

Hultural differences. On December 6, 2010, a newsreader on BBC Radio 4 meant to introduce an upcoming guest, "Jeremy Hunt, the Culture Secretary" of the U.K. But he transposed the "c" in "culture" with the "h" in Hunt. What followed was roughly thirty seconds of the host trying to continue with the story, in between nervous coughs, several long pauses, suppressed giggles, and more pretend coughs—he even said at one point, "Sorry, coughing fit"—before more suppressed giggles could be heard, until he finally got it together and continued on with his show. (Including the interview with Jeremy Hunt.) The host apologized later in the episode, saying, "I'm very sorry to anyone who thought it wasn't what they wanted to hear over their breakfast. Neither did I, needless to say." The host's name: James Naughtie.

Later that day, Andrew Marr, host of Radio 4's *Start the Week* program, had a panel of guests on to discuss Naughtie's naughty slip of the tongue, along with "Freudian slips" in general, and promised listeners he wouldn't be making one himself. He, too, then transposed the "c" in "culture" and the "h" in "Hunt."

Bomer boner. In October 2009 actor Matt Bomer of the USA Network drama *White Collar* was on *The Today Show*. Host Jenna Wolfe introduced him as "Matt Boner."

Hoosier what now? In December 2011, meteorologist Ashton Altieri of 9News in Denver, Colorado, said to anchor Aaron Matas, "Congratulations on your big hooters." (He meant to say, "Congratulations on your big Hoosiers win," referring to Matas's home-state Indiana Hoosiers basketball team.)

Just plain nuts. In February 2009, CNN's Zain Verjee told viewers that Northwest Airlines "began serving penis this month." Further on in the story she informed them that "Georgia is the top penis producing state in the country." She had meant to say—twice— "peanuts."

WHO'S THAT GUY?

In a May 2006 financial news segment of *BBC News*, presenter Karen Bowerman introduced a piece about online music. The camera cut away from Bowerman to a man sitting on a stool as Bowerman said, "Well, Guy Kewney is editor of the technology website NewsWireless." As Bowerman said those words, the man on camera went wide-eyed, his mouth opened in a big O-shape, and he generally looked like he was about to swallow his tongue.

The man in the stool was not Guy Kewney—he was Guy Goma, who had come by BBC to apply for an IT job. Bowerman's producer had been sent to get Kewney, had seen Goma, asked him if his name was "Guy." Goma naturally answered in the affirmative, and he was ushered into the studio. The very best part of this story: Goma decided to go along with it. He actually answered Bowerman's questions—even though he had no idea what he was talking about.

As soon as the interview was over, Goma explained what had happened—but the segment had been aired live, so there was nothing to be done. The real Guy Kewney—who was in a reception room where had been told to wait—had watched the interview on a TV there in a state of confusion.

FAULTY RESEARCH

In 2001 NASA launched *Genesis*, a space probe used to sample and observe the solar wind. It successfully took samples and retrieved data, but as it reentered Earth's atmosphere in 2004, its landing parachute failed to deploy, and the capsule smashed to the ground. The reason for the failure: Two acceleration sensors had been installed backward in the $260 million device.

• NASA launched the *Mars Climate Orbiter* in December 1998 to study the weather and atmosphere of Mars. The probe was supposed to collect data and radio it back to NASA control centers in Florida. It never happened. That's because the software used to control the *Orbiter* were entered in U.S. measurements (inches, feet)—they were supposed to be in metric. As a result, the *Orbiter* missed its atmospheric entry point and entered too late, burning up on reentry in September 1999. Total cost of the failed mission: $655 million.

• Funded by a generous government grant, the Institute for Animal Health in Scotland spent 1996 to 2001 attempting to determine if mad cow disease was able to cross over from cattle brains to sheep brains. They mainly analyzed and dissected sheep brains they'd suspected had been infected. The program was halted in late 2001 when the scientists realized that the whole time they had been studying cow brains instead of sheep brains.

• "Acoustic Kitty" was a top-secret CIA project in the 1960s in which government scientists surgically implanted a cat with batteries and ran an antenna through its tail. The goal: Plant the cat near enemy offices and have it transmit conversations to a receiving station. Before the first cat could be used in the field, it was hit by a car.

YOU'RE FIRED

In 2010 Gene Cranick's home in rural Obion County, Tennessee, caught fire. Cranick got out of the house, then called the fire department. But fire trucks never came and Cranick's house burned down. Why? Obion County isn't large enough to support its own fire department, so residents rely on the emergency services of nearby South Fulton. The trade-off? A $75 annual emergency services coverage fee. Cranick hadn't paid his fee, so his house burned to the ground.

PUT A RING IN IT

Reed Harris and his girlfriend, Kaitlin Whipple, liked to eat at Wendy's. So when he decided to propose marriage, the fast-food place was the obvious, if nontraditional, place to do it. Harris, Whipple, and some friends went to Wendy's one night, with the friends there to record the momentous proposal on their camera phones. Harris's clever idea: hide the ring in Whipple's Frosty, Wendy's extra-thick milkshake beverage.

Everyone sat and waited for Whipple to bite into something hard during one of those Frosty spoonfuls...but it never happened. The rest of the party told Whipple to finish up her cup fast, and she did. No ring.

After a quick trip to the hospital, Harris proposed to Whipple holding up not the engagement ring but an X-ray of Whipple's stomach with a diamond ring clearly visible in her stomach. (Whipple eventually passed the ring, which she still wears, because she actually married Harris.)

YOU'RE GONNA DIE

Up to 40 people are killed each year by jellyfish. And that's just in the Philippines.

• Don't grumble when your seat assignment is way in the back of the plane, in crying-baby class. In the event of a crash landing, the rich folks up front in first class are most likely to die.

• According to England's *Daily Mirror*, "More than 2,500 left-handed people are killed every year around the world from using equipment meant for right-handed people. The right-handed power saw is the most deadly item."

• Each year roughly 1,000 Americans die because they insist on texting or talking on a cell phone while driving. According to a Virginia Tech study, if you text while you drive, your risk of collision is 23 times greater than if you were paying attention.

• Hippos kill 2,900 people a year in Africa. In the U.S., that number is virtually zero...because there are no hippos native to the U.S. But there are dogs in the U.S., and dog attacks take about 35 American lives each year.

• The press sure had a field day after *Kill Bill* star David Carradine was killed in 2009 by "autoerotic asphyxiation" (which involves pulleys and gags and other such strange apparatuses). Carradine wasn't alone (well, at the time he was). More than 1,000 people die each year from these kind of sexual mishaps.

• On average, two Americans are killed by vending machines each year.

• Approximately 450 Americans die annually after falling out of bed. Most are very young, very old, or very drunk.

• They don't feel very safe, but the rate of injury and fatalities on roller coasters don't lie: 900 million rides are taken each year, with only about 7,300 injuries...and 10 deaths. So buckle up and keep your hands and feet inside the car.

• Of course, the leading cause of dying is death. The Grim Reaper takes away about 57 million people worldwide each year. That means that today, 155,000 of your fellow humans will perish. A dozen or so died while you read this sentence.

THE ROYAL MISTAKE

After years of risky loans, a "hands-off" regulation policy, and other factors, by 2008 the Royal Bank of Scotland was in such bad shape that it needed a $70 billion bailout from the UK government. RBS tried numerous ways to right the ship, including a computer upgrade and outsourcing jobs to India. Both strategies are usually good for helping a company grow. But not always.

On June 19, 2012, a technician in Hyderabad, India, was updating software when he made a mistake. While working in a database that held the entire day's transactions, he hit delete. Before the problem was noticed, he deleted two more days of transactions. Bank records for 17 million accounts were gone. Customers went days without access to their money; some had to wait 10 weeks. Even companies without RBS accounts were affected, like mortgage and utility companies that received automatic payments from RBS customers.

The error could ultimately cost the bank $3 billion, including reimbursement of late fees and overdraft charges, overtime for 7,000 employees, even hotel fees for customers who were kicked out of their homes after rent checks bounced.

BLOOD ON THE SCREEN

*T**wilight Zone: The Movie** (1983)*

A horrific hallucination scene set during the Vietnam War involved both night shooting and a low-flying helicopter. Lead actor Vic Morrow and two child actors were crushed and decapitated after the pilot lost control and crashed into them. Director John Landis and several others involved in the production were tried and acquitted on charges of manslaughter. As a result of the tragedy, many movie studios avoided helicopter stunts in the years that followed, and several regulations to protect child actors were substantially revised.

Troy (2004)

In this swords-and-sandals flick, Brad Pitt played Achilles, the Greek warrior who died after his heel was hit by an arrow. Appropriately enough, Pitt injured his foot while filming a fight scene with co-star Eric Bana. The sequence required Pitt to leap and hit Bana's shield with a spear. But Pitt landed wrong, rupturing one of his Achilles tendons in the process. Production continued during Pitt's recuperation, which took three months. When Pitt's ankle was healthy, the crew celebrated by filming the scene where his character is undone by his delicate heel.

Top Gun (1986)

This action-packed blockbuster featured several tricky air stunts. Professional stuntman and pilot Art Scholl, whose credits included *The A-Team* and *The Right Stuff*, was brought on board to perform many of them. During the filming of a flight maneuver called a "flat spin," Scholl's plane began losing altitude and he radioed, "I have a problem...I have a real problem." He was unable to regain control and crashed off the coast of Southern California. Neither the aircraft nor Scholl's remains were ever recovered, and the cause of the accident was never determined. The film was dedicated to his memory.

The Crow (1994)

The set of this supernatural action film was infamously problem-plagued, if not downright cursed. Star Brandon Lee, the son of martial arts legend Bruce Lee, died from injuries sustained after being shot with a prop gun that had been mistakenly loaded with live ammunition. Earlier in the production, a carpenter survived life-threatening electrical burns after the crane he was operating came into contact with high-voltage power lines. A disgruntled carpenter seeking revenge against the film's producers (he'd been fired) drove his car through the studio's plaster shop. If all of this wasn't bad enough, a crew member accidentally drove a screwdriver through his own hand, and a stuntman fell through one of the set's roofs.

Gothika (2003)

This psychological thriller didn't feature a lot of stunt work, but Halle Berry still managed to break her arm. Co-star Robert Downey Jr. was supposed to grab her arm and twist it. Unfortunately, he twisted too hard and Berry's arm snapped. The production had to shut down for eight weeks while Berry recovered.

The Sorcerer's Apprentice (2010)

Several scenes in this Nicolas Cage movie were shot on the streets of New York City. During the filming of a chase scene, a stuntman driving a Ferrari lost control of the vehicle while attempting to perform a "power slide." The car slid too far, jumped a curb, took out an electrical pole, and careened through the entrance of a Sbarro restaurant in the middle of Times Square. Two people were injured, one of whom was hit by the pole. Two nights later, another nine onlookers were hurt when a stunt driver lost control of a BMW X5 after she slammed into a parked SUV. Many crew members began to wonder if the film was cursed while media reports questioned why the sidewalks around the set weren't closed to pedestrians. The producers later blamed both accidents on inclement weather and slippery pavement.

"NINE ONLOOKERS WERE HURT WHEN A STUNT DRIVER LOST CONTROL OF A BMW X5 AFTER SHE SLAMMED INTO A PARKED SUV."

THE HUNTER WHO BURNED CALIFORNIA

I n October 2003, 33-year-old Sergio Martinez was in the forests outside San Diego hunting for deer when he got separated from his hunting partner. Not wanting to scare away the deer, Martinez didn't call out for help. Despite the dry conditions that are common in California, he lit a rescue flare.

The Department of Fire Protection reacted almost immediately. After 30 minutes, the fire was still smaller than a football field, and 320 firefighters were at work. But then Santa Ana winds picked up. Within 14 hours, the fire had spread 30 miles.

Martinez was saved, but the Cedar Fire, as it came to be known, took over a week to contain. It became the largest wildfire in California history, eventually destroying an area larger than the city of Los Angeles. More than 2,200 homes were burned, and 14 people died. The fire cost the state $1.3 billion, but Martinez avoided jail time. Instead, he was sentenced to six months of work release, a five-year probation, and a fine of $9,000, to be paid to the U.S. Forest Service and used in their fire safety education program.

ARE YOU READY FOR SOME FOOTBALL (FAILS)?

Whizzed. During a 1952 NFL game between the Chicago Bears and the Los Angeles Rams, Bears halfback Wilford "Whizzer" White tried to avoid the rush by running backward, dodging defenders, a bit more, and a little bit more, until he had run 51 yards—the wrong way—to his own goal line. Then he fumbled the ball and the Rams scored.

Caught with his punts down. During the 1986 NFC Championship Game, New York Giants punter Sean Landeta attempted a routine punt...and missed. He kicked his own leg instead of the ball. The Chicago Bears' Shaun Gayle scooped up the ball and ran it back for a touchdown. (Landeta blamed the whiffed punt—the only one in NFL history—on a gust of wind.) The Giants lost the game 21–0.

Gus what? Washington Redskins quarterback Gus Frerotte scored on a 1-yard touchdown run just before halftime of a 1997 game, and was so excited he headbutted the wall under the stands... and sprained his neck. He finished out the half, but spent the rest of the day in the hospital.

Party foul. Arizona Cardinals rookie kicker Bill Gramatica made a 43-yard field goal during a 2001 game against the New York Giants, then jumped into the air in celebration, landed awkwardly, and tore a ligament in his right knee. He was out for the rest of the season.

Falling Starr. At an NFL dinner the evening before Super Bowl XXXIII in January 1999, Atlanta Falcons safety Eugene Robinson was awarded the Bart Starr Award, given annually to a player with "high moral character." Later that night, Robinson was arrested for attempting to solicit a prostitute. Robinson was allowed to play in the Super Bowl the next day (he and the Falcons lost to the Denver Broncos 34–19), but he had to return the award.

Duke of Owww. After running for a touchdown during a game in 2005, Maynard "Duke" Pettijohn of the Arena Football League's Dallas Desperados emphatically spiked the football...and the entire audience let out a dramatic (and sympathetic) "Ohhhhh!" The ball had bounced straight up into the groin of referee Mike DeLaney, who fell to the ground in agony. Pettijohn was given a (very) personal foul.

CELEBRATE GOOD TIMES! *COME ON!*

Celebrate Good Times: In September 2012, a teenager from Haren, in the Netherlands, invited her friends to her 16th birthday party via Facebook.

Come On: She forgot to mark the invitation "private." Strangers saw the message and shared it, and it quickly went viral...roughly 4,000 people showed up for the party. The girl and her family had to be taken from their home by police to an undisclosed location as the revelers took to the streets of Haren, smashing shop windows, setting cars ablaze, and engaging in skirmishes with the more than 500 police officers called in to deal with the party/riot. Twenty-nine people were injured, and 34 were arrested.

Celebrate Good Times: Alex Bowden attended a party in a Darwin, Australia, suburb in August 2012. Fireworks were set off at some point in the festivities.

Come On: Bowden, thinking it would be a good party trick, pulled down his trousers, placed a spinning "Flying Bee" firecracker between his butt cheeks, and lit it. Partygoers called paramedics when the firecracker went off—and Bowden began screaming in agony. He was rushed to a hospital to be treated for "quite severe and very painful burns to his cheeks, back, and private bits." (Bowden also burned his fingers...when he pulled the still-spinning and burning incendiary device from his butt.) From his hospital bed the day after the incident, Bowden said, "It's not as bad as everyone's saying," and added that his mother "thought it was funny."

Celebrate Good Times: On December 31, 2010, a man in Munich, Germany, drove to the center of the city to take part in raucous New Year's Eve festivities. He got very, very drunk. In the wee hours of the morning he very responsibly got a taxi home, and the next day went to retrieve his car.

Come On: He couldn't find his car. He called the police and they helped him look for it—he remembered the area where he had parked it but they couldn't find the car, either. Days went by—no car. Weeks went by—no car. Then months went by. Still no car. Worse: He was a master woodworker, and his tools—more than $50,000 worth—were in the car's trunk. Finally, in October 2012—almost two years later—a police officer found the woodworker's lost car. It had been sitting right where he'd left it...about 2.5 miles from where he had told police he was sure he'd parked it. His tools were still in the trunk.

DELETE THE TWEET

PARDON MY FRENCH. During an early round at the 2012 London Summer Olympics, Switzerland's men's soccer team lost to South Korea 2-1. Later that day, Swiss player Michel Morganella posted a message on Twitter. The translation, from French: "I'm going to beat up every Korean, go on, burn yourselves, bunch of mongoloids." Morganella was immediately kicked off the Swiss national team and sent home. He later apologized and said he had been "provoked" into the reaction by other Twitter users. His Twitter account was soon deleted.

HUGH JASSMAN. Australian-born Hollywood star Hugh Jackman was visiting his home country in April 2009 when he tweeted, "Having lunch on the harbor across from the Opera Center. Loving life!" Several of Jackman's Australian fans called foul: "Harbor" is spelled "harbour" in Australia, and "center" is spelled "centre." Jackman initially made things worse by blaming the mistakes on his smartphone's auto-correct spelling function—but his fans called foul again: Even if he had spelled "centre" correctly, it's not called the Opera Centre—it's the Opera House. Jackman finally admitted that he hadn't made the tweets—a staffer back in Los Angeles had. He apologized for lying.

YOU'RE HIRED! YOU'RE FIRED! In February 2009, someone with the Twitter handle "@theconnor" posted a tweet celebrating—sort of—a new job: "Cisco just offered me a job!" @theconnor wrote. "Now I have to weigh the utility of a fatty paycheck against the daily commute to San Jose and hating the work." A short while later Tim Lavad—a Cisco employee—responded: "Who is the hiring manager? I'm sure they would love to know that you will hate the work." The exchange went viral, and the person Twitter users dubbed "Cisco Fatty" was mocked mercilessly by thousands of twitterers before the tweet was finally deleted and the account made private. "Cisco Fatty" was later revealed to be 22-year-old Connor Riley, a student at the University of California, Berkeley. She admitted that Cisco had indeed learned about her errant tweet—and had rescinded the job offer. "I should have been a little bit more careful," she said.

WHAT A BOOB! In November 2011, Dean McDermott, husband of actress Tori Spelling, took a photo of the couple's five-year-old son with a silly sticker on his face and posted it for his 80,000 Twitter followers. And they started retweeting the photo like crazy. Why? McDermott had failed to notice that his wife's naked breasts were plainly visible in the photo's background. McDermott deleted the tweet not much later, but it was too late. An embarrassed Spelling later told CNN that it had been an honest accident: "I am a mom, I was nursing my baby," she said. (The couple had just had their third child a month earlier.)

IT'S A RECORD, ALMOST!

Mower riding: Floyd Malacek tried to jump the Lac qui Parle River in Minnesota while riding on lawn mower. It's a 40-foot jump. Malacek missed...by 35 feet.

Live burial: On April 1, 1977, Robert Mannah had himself buried in a box underground, intending to stay for 102 days in order to claim the world record for a live burial. On day 102 he emerged, only to find out that he made a miscalculation—the record was 217 days, not 101. He also found out that Guinness had long since discontinued the live-burial category because it was too dangerous.

Assembly of Smurfs: In 2008, 395 Croatians gathered together, painted their faces blue, and donned long-sleeved blue shirts, white pants, and white caps to set the record for "most Smurfs gathered together at one time." Official photos were taken and sent to Guinness for inclusion and certification in the next book of world records. After all, they had smashed the previous record (it existed) of 291 human-Smurfs. However, they hadn't done very good research, because in late 2007, students at Warwick

> **"GUINNESS HAD LONG SINCE DISCONTINUED THE LIVE-BURIAL CATEGORY BECAUSE IT WAS TOO DANGEROUS."**

University in England had also smashed the record, as well as the Croatians' attempt: 451 Smurfs. "We read on the Internet that the record was 290 people held by a group of Americans, and decided to beat it. We could easily have got more Smurfs, but we thought that over a hundred more than the American record would be enough," said a dejected, or downright blue, Croatian Smurf.

Staying awake: Tony Wright of Cornwell set what he thought was a world record for sleeplessness by a two-hour margin, when in 2007, he stayed awake for 266 hours. Then he found out that his research had been wrong, and someone else had set a record of 276 hours. And then he found out that Guinness no longer lists records for sleep deprivation.

Coconut smashing: In 2008, a Danish man wanted to set the world record for opening coconuts with his bare hands. He planned a public record-breaking ceremony in Copenhagen, and invited a TV crew and representatives from Guinness. The man stood in front of a table stocked with a row of 20 coconuts. The timer went off and off he went, chopping at the coconuts with only his hand. He missed the first one completely. The second one he hit, and it didn't crack. Same thing with the next eight coconuts. At that point, the man gave up, fairly certain he'd broken his hand. Number of coconuts busted open: zero.

STAFF INFECTION

In late 17th-century France, Jean-Baptiste Lully was King Louis XIV's favorite dancer and composer...until he "baroque" his foot. Lully was one of the first composers to lead an orchestra with a baton. But this wasn't like today's tiny batons, waved all about. A baton back then was a really big stick—six feet long with a brass point on the bottom, more like a staff—that the conductor would pound on the floor to help the musicians keep time.

One night in 1687, during a celebratory performance (the king had just recovered from a long illness), Lully was exuberantly banging his big stick on the floor over and over while the orchestra played. He got

"HIS WOUND WAS BAD, BUT SURVIVABLE."

so caught up in the moment that he stabbed his big toe with the baton. Lully screamed in pain as the crowd recoiled in horror. The performance came to an abrupt end. But not Lully: His wound was bad, but survivable. The king's doctors, noting that gangrene would soon spread upward from the abscess, attempted to amputate Lully's toe. But the composer protested (he was a dancer, too, after all), and fought off the doctors and their saws. The gangrene spread, and Lully died a slow, painful death.

THE COCAINE AMPUTATION

Cocaine, a powdered extract of the coca leaf, has been used as a recreational drug for more than a century. It makes users incredibly alert, but it also makes their hearts beat faster, potentially leading to stroke, heart attack, or sudden death. In the 1970s and '80s, it gained popularity as a sexual-enhancement drug—people wouldn't just ingest it, they would rub it on or inject it into their genitals to concentrate the drug's powerful effects.

In a report in a 1988 issue of the *Journal of the American Medical Association*, three doctors wrote about an (unnamed) man who experienced the worst cocaine side effects imaginable (death may or may not be worse). The 34-year-old New York City man told doctors that on occasion, he injected a cocaine solution directly into his urethra through the tip of his penis. It had no ill effects, until he did it before a romantic encounter in June 1987. Afterward, his erection didn't go away for three days (a medical condition called priapism). He

> **"PEOPLE WOULDN'T JUST INGEST IT, THEY WOULD RUB IT ON OR INJECT IT INTO THEIR GENITALS TO CONCENTRATE THE DRUG'S POWERFUL EFFECTS."**

sought medical attention, and doctors were able to drain his penis of blood.

The problem was that the blood went inward, not outward. The blood, full of cocaine and bacteria, coursed throughout his body. From there it coagulated under the man's skin, leading to blood clots in his genitals, arms, legs, back, and chest, and gangrene in his legs, fingers, and penis. Twelve days later, doctors had to amputate both of the man's legs, nine fingers...and his penis.

E.T., GO HOME

It's one of the most famous parts of one of the most popular movies of all time. In the 1982 blockbuster *E.T. the Extra-Terrestrial,* Elliott (Henry Thomas) lures the alien out of a hiding place with a trail of bite-size Reese's candies.

It wasn't the first-ever instance of "product placement," but it's certainly among the most high-profile, and it put the practice on the radar of the general public. What's more is that it worked—in June 1982, shortly after the release of the movie, sales of Reese's Pieces went up by 65 percent.

The loser in the story: Mars candy company. Producers of *E.T.* went to Mars first, wanting Elliott's candy of choice to be M&M's. Despite the fact that the movie looked like it was going to be a hit—and Steven Spielberg was directing it—Mars turned down the chance to pay to put M&M's in the film. Why? The company had already allocated its entire advertising budget for the year.

> **"PRODUCERS OF *E.T.* WENT TO MARS FIRST, WANTING ELLIOTT'S CANDY OF CHOICE TO BE M&M'S."**

GENITAL WARFARE

MY OLD VIRGINNY HOME
An elderly North Carolina woman arrived at the ER saying she had green vines growing in her "virginny," as she quaintly called it. An exam and a few X-rays confirmed her story: It was a vine, and it had sprouted...out of a potato. The woman explained that her uterus had prolapsed, or fallen out (a condition not uncommon in elderly women), so she'd popped in a potato to hold it up—and forgotten about it.

VERY BAD KITTY
A panicked woman brought her unconscious boyfriend into the ER and explained that she'd found him lying in the bathtub. Doctors noted a large lump on the man's head...and some curious scratches on his scrotum. As they were trying to determine what happened, the man woke up and told his story: He'd been cleaning his tub in the nude, and while kneeling to scrub the drain, he didn't realize that his swaying testicles had drawn the attention of his cat. The cat pounced, and the man jumped in pain...then hit his head on the tiles and knocked himself out.

SAY WHAT?

In August 2003, Valdemar Lopes de Moraes of Monte Claros, Brazil, walked into a medical clinic to get treated for an earache. A few hours later he walked out—with a vasectomy. What happened? The nurses called "*Aldemar*" (for a vasectomy), and Valdemar thought he'd been called. "The strangest thing," said the clinic manager, "is that he asked no questions when the doctor started preparations in the area which had so little to do with his ear. He later explained that he thought it was an ear inflammation that got down to his testicles."

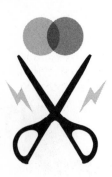

LOVE MACHINE

In a 1991 issue of the journal *Medical Aspects of Human Sexuality*, a urologist from West Chester, Pennsylvania, wrote about an ER patient he'd treated for a lacerated and swollen scrotum. At a checkup appointment, the man admitted how he'd gotten the injury: He'd been pleasuring himself by holding his genitals against the canvas belt on a piece of industrial equipment at his machine shop (during his lunch hour, because otherwise it would have been weird). He pressed against it too hard. It gets worse: He tried to close the wound himself...with an industrial staple gun.

WEIRD (AND REAL) CELL-PHONE INSURANCE CLAIMS

A couple filed a claim for a new phone after they lost theirs while on a cruise ship. They had dropped the phone into the ocean, they said, while trying to take a photo of themselves attempting to reenact Leonardo DiCaprio and Kate Winslet's "I'm the king of the world!" scene from the film *Titanic*.

• A woman from Liverpool, England, filed for a new phone because, she said, hers had a crack in it. After discovering that her boyfriend was cheating on her, she explained, she threw the phone at his head. He ducked—and the phone hit a wall and broke.

• A woman from Bristol, England, filed a claim to have the cost of a new BlackBerry Bold 9900 reimbursed because she had worn out the phone's vibrator function with, uh, intimate use.

• A construction worker applied for a replacement phone when his fell out of his back pocket just as he was sitting down..."on the loo." Unfortunately, he didn't notice...and went about his business, so to speak. He didn't know the phone was missing from his pocket until he saw it in the toilet bowl.

MUSICIAN BOMBS

Wayne Coyne is the front man of the Flaming Lips, a popular arty rock band. They've done a lot of kooky things over the years, including releasing a four-album set designed to be played all at once, and performing onstage encased in a bubble. But in November 2012, Coyne was flying out of Oklahoma City (his hometown) to Houston, Texas, when he was stopped at a security checkpoint. An X-ray scan alerted officials to contraband inside his luggage. Drugs? Guns? Nope—a grenade. When questioned by NSA workers Coyne said he had taken it from a party in Arkansas a week earlier but that it was not a live grenade and that it was painted gold. In other words it was a piece of art and he took it because he thought it was interesting.

"DRUGS? GUNS? NOPE— A GRENADE."

The TSA wasn't going to take any chances. They detained Coyne...and shut down the Will Rogers Airport in Oklahoma City for several hours. By the time all was clear, hundreds of people had missed their flights. Coyne posted an apology on Twitter along with a picture of himself in the airport flashing a peace sign.

FLAMEOUTS

After William Bonner, 36, awoke in the intensive care unit, he told police officers that his face had been burned by some thugs at a bar in Augusta, Georgia. The surveillance video told a different story: Bonner's friends had burned his face. He told them to. He even bet them that he would let them do it. His buddy poured a shot of rum on Bonner's head and tried to light it. It wouldn't light, so he tried again. That did the trick. Bonner's world went up in flames as he screamed and ran wildly around the bar. His friends laughed and called him "Ghost Rider." Once they realized he was in serious trouble, they called an ambulance.

• **When Johnny Knoxville set himself on fire** on the MTV show *Jackass* (he was roasted on a rotisserie spit), he was shown first putting on a flame-retardant suit. A message was displayed onscreen in big letters that informed viewers Knoxville was wearing a flame-retardant suit. He said, "I am wearing a flame-retardant suit. Do not try this at home." Within days of the episode's airing, at least two preteen boys did try it at home. Neither wore a flame-retardant suit. Both received severe burns. One of the burned boys even appeared on *Good Morning America* just so he could blame Johnny Knoxville for giving him the idea.

• **Poor Gary Allen Banning.** He made the all-too-common mistake of accidentally taking a swig from a jar of gasoline and then lighting a cigarette. He was 43.

• **Christine Mecca, 51, of Ford City, Pennsylvania, accidentally lit herself on fire** at a gas station. At the hospital, Mecca first blamed the flames on a lit cigarette, but then confessed to what really happened: She told police she had accidentally set herself on fire while trying to set fire to a letter from her boss informing her that she had been fired.

• **A 51-year-old drunk man from Kamloops, British Columbia**, passed out in a grassy field one night with a lit cigarette in his mouth. When he awoke, he was on fire. So was the field. He got up and ran away while trying to brush off the flames. Then he got on a bike and tried to ride farther away from the fire. That's when he got hit by a train. When he awoke on the tracks, he had severe burns and a big gash on his head (from the train). Later, at the hospital, his bad day was made worse when he got arrested for starting the fire. Then he was charged with theft for stealing the bike.

• **Thanks to the thousands of surveillance cameras in England,** there's a lot of great footage of Brits embarrassing themselves. One such Brit is Michael Morgan. In 2012 a sidewalk security camera recorded him as he rode his bike up to the entrance of a pub that he'd been ejected from the night before for fighting. Seeking sweet revenge, the 33-year-old (still on his bike) doused the door with gasoline and lit it on fire. Then he rode away, seemingly unaware of the flames leaping up his legs and back. Morgan escaped without serious injury (as did the pub), but he was easily recognized from the security footage and arrested soon after. He was sentenced to two and a half years in prison. The landlord of the adjacent building pointed out that karma goes far beyond a mere prison sentence: "People will always remember Michael Morgan as the clown on the bike who set himself on fire."

ALWAYS HAVE A BACKUP PLAN

Sweden's King Gustavus Adolphus refused to wear armor at the 1632 Battle of Lützen, a decisive battle in the Thirty Years' War, between the Swedish Protestant Union and the Catholic League. The king claimed that "The Lord God is my armor." Then he got shot and died.

DIG IT!

Until the 1980s, Lake Peigneur was a popular fishing spot for sportsmen in Louisiana. The areas around and beneath the lake were also popular, having been mined for salt and tapped by oil companies. At least they were until November 21, 1980, when a petroleum-seeking drill from a Texaco platform plunged through the lake. Unfortunately, a member of the company's crew made a critical miscalculation. Instead of hitting a deposit filled with Texas Tea, the drill pierced a mine shaft beneath the lake owned by the Diamond Crystal Salt Company.

The crew realized that something was wrong when they tried to free the drill and it wouldn't budge. The platform began to tilt and a series of loud pops filled the air. They fled to shore as thousands of gallons of water surged into the ruptured mine shaft.

"THOUSANDS OF GALLONS OF WATER SURGED INTO THE RUPTURED MINE SHAFT."

As the hole grew bigger and bigger, Junius Gaddison, an electrician working in the mines, heard a series of strange noises. He went to investigate and suddenly found himself knee-deep in muddy water. He sounded an alarm, sending the mine's 50-man crew rushing for the nearest exit route to the surface: a slow-moving elevator that could hold only eight people at a time.

Meanwhile up top, the small hole created by the drill became a mile-wide whirlpool that sucked the drilling platform down into the mine while the intense air pressure in the mine caused a series of 400-foot-tall geysers to burst out of the ground. The awesome sucking power of the whirlpool could not be abated: Over the following hours, it gobbled up a second drilling platform, a loading dock, a parking lot, and over 70 acres of terrain. So much water filled the mine that the Delcambre Canal, which typically empties the lake into the bay, began to flow backward, pulling 11 barges into the spinning vortex.

After three hours, Lake Peigneur had lost all of its 3.5 billion gallons of water. Then saltwater from the canal started flowing into the empty pit where the lake once sat, creating what would temporarily be the tallest waterfall in Louisiana. It reached a height of 164 feet and flowed for a day or two before the canal refilled the lake with water from Vermilion Bay. Eventually, nine of the sunken barges popped back up to the lake's surface. The tugboat and the drilling platforms are still trapped in the destroyed mine.

Amazingly enough, the accident didn't cause a single human fatality or even an injury. All 55 miners managed to escape to shore before the whirlpool's current became too strong. Texaco was later required to pay around $45 million in out-of-court settlements.

REAL ANSWERS FROM *FAMILY FEUD*

Host: "Tell me a slang word for money."
Contestant: "Money."

Host: "Name a state that begins with the letter N."
Contestant: "Mexico."

Host: "Name a candy bar that might describe your mate in bed."
Contestant: "Butterfinger."

Host: "Tell me a food that comes in instant form."
Contestant: "Asparagus."

Host: "Besides a bird, name something in a birdcage."
Contestant: "Hamster."

Host: "Name a noisy bird."
Contestant: "Chipmunk."

Host: "Name a way of cooking fish."
Contestant: "Cod."

Host: "Name something a man might have in his pants when he's going on a hot date."
Contestant: "A boner."

Host: "Name something a burglar would not want to see in your house."
Contestant: "Naked grandma!"

Host: "Name something a blind person might use."
Contestant: "A sword."

FLAMIN' HOT HEALTH CRISIS AVERTED

As part of the ongoing fight against childhood obesity, many school districts nationwide have banned vending machines and junk foods that lack nutritional value. Singled out for omission in New Mexico, California, and Illinois: Flamin' Hot Cheetos, a variety of the cheese-powder-coated corn-based snack that is also covered with a spicy-hot red powder. In addition to providing a delicious carbohydrate boost, Flamin' Hot Cheetos stain the eater's fingers red (as opposed to the orange fingers provided by traditional Cheetos).

"THAT FOOD DYE TENDS TO SEEP INTO FECES."

Flamin' Hot Cheetos get their distinctive red hue from a large amount of food dye. That food dye tends to seep into feces, leading to anecdotal reports around the country of panicked parents bringing their children to doctors' offices and emergency rooms because they have bloody stools, a symptom of a number of terrifying medical conditions. Thankfully, more often not, it's just red poop brought on by a bag of red-hot Cheetos.

DISCO INFERNO

The only cultural force as strong as disco in the late 1970s was the "disco sucks" movement, adhered to by those tired of disco. Feelings reached their peak on July 12, 1979: "Disco Demolition Night," a promotion that was part of a Chicago White Sox doubleheader at Comiskey Park. It was orchestrated by Chicago disc jockey Steve Dahl, who had lost his job when his rock station changed its format to disco. Between games, Dahl planned to blow up a massive pile of disco records. The White Sox hired security for an expected crowd of about 35,000. Instead, 60,000 people showed up, and started demolishing disco a little early, throwing records at each other and at the players on the field.

When the intermission finally came, Dahl drove a Jeep around the field as the crowd chanted "Disco sucks!" Then Dahl used dynamite to detonate crates full of more than 1,000 disco records. The explosion ripped a giant hole in the turf and sent vinyl everywhere. Players fled into the dugouts while fans jumped the fences and further vandalized the field, stealing bases and toppling a batting cage. The White Sox had to forfeit the second game.

THE FASHION CAFÉ

Among the biggest pop-culture crazes of the early '90s were theme restaurant chains, like the rock music–themed Hard Rock Café and the movie-themed Planet Hollywood. Both of those eateries are still around, but not at the peak of where they were 20 years ago. The 1990s were also the time of the model as celebrity—"supermodels" such as Cindy Crawford and Linda Evangelista were the epitome of glamour and success. The Fashion Café is where these two fads came together.

The Fashion Café was the misguided brainchild of Tommaso Buti and his brother Francesco, Italian entrepreneurs who moved to New York City in the early '90s. After making connections in the fashion industry and developing friendships with Hollywood stars like Kevin Costner, the Butis tried to cash in on both the popularity of theme restaurants and the supermodel craze. The Butis convinced supermodels Elle MacPherson, Claudia Schiffer, Naomi Campbell, and Christy Turlington to come on board. The models agreed to make public appearances to promote the Fashion Café in exchange for big paychecks and a percentage of the profits if the enterprise was a success. With their names attached, attracting investors wasn't a problem.

The first Fashion Café, located in Manhattan's Rockefeller Center, opened its doors in 1995, and plans were already under way for a second location in London. The New York grand opening was a star-studded event that captured headlines around the world. But mediocre reviews, a lack of repeat business, and weird events like fashion shows featuring unknown models strutting around in pajamas didn't bode well for the franchise's future. While the Butis opened additional locations in the UK, South Africa, Mexico, and Spain, they quickly took on serious debts. There was simply no escaping the fact that the chain was doomed to failure—not to mention the irony of the restaurant's fare of cheeseburgers and steaks pitched by representatives of the fashion industry, synonymous with an aversion to food.

> "UNKNOWN MODELS STRUTTING AROUND IN PAJAMAS DIDN'T BODE WELL FOR THE FRANCHISE'S FUTURE."

In 1998 tax agents began sniffing around the New York location's financial records, and utility companies and others began hounding the Butis for late payments. Meanwhile, Turlington and Schiffer pulled out, publicly blaming old vendettas with Campbell. While their empire crumbled, the Buti brothers developed a taste for the high life. Tommaso moved into a $25,000-a-month apartment and threw himself an elaborate birthday party at a Manhattan hot spot. The duo also began digging into the Café's coffers, spending tons of money on fancy cars and other luxuries. They even managed to ring up $132,000 in cell phone bills, all on the chain's dime. With investors fuming and bill collectors circling the now-closed flagship in New York, Tommaso resigned as CEO in September 1998. In December 2000, the federal government filed 51 charges against the Butis for fraud and other crimes. Tommaso was later arrested in Italy, and his brother went on the run. All told, the Butis reportedly stole over $12 million from their investors.

TWO CIVIC GOOFS

• In the 1990s, Cleveland had a labor contract with its transit workers that called for any train driver who was fired to be rehired as a bus driver. In 1991 Lynne Herron got a job as a Cleveland bus driver after she caused an accident that injured 14 people during her old job as a train driver. The crash was caused by a disengaged safety system, which had been purposely disengaged...by Herron.

• To save money in 1974, the city council of Bramber, England, voted to shut off their streetlights for three days. The experiment saved Bramber £11.59 in electricity costs. However, the city spent £18.48 on a shutoff fee, then another £12 to turn the lights on. Final tally: It *cost* Bramber £18.89 to go without streetlights.

WHO NEEDS TELEVISION?

Shelley Long was virtually unknown when she was cast as intellectual barmaid Diane Chambers on *Cheers* in 1982. The show went on to become a huge hit, and Long won an Emmy. She balanced her *Cheers* shooting schedule with starring roles in a string of hit films, including *Outrageous Fortune* and *The Money Pit*. In 1987 Long left *Cheers* to focus solely on movies. *Cheers* replaced her with a new character, bar manager Rebecca Howe, portrayed by Kirstie Alley. With Alley, *Cheers* became the #1 show on TV. Long's movie career never quite jelled. (Remember *The Boyfriend School*? *Frozen Assets*?) Long later returned to TV with a string of made-for-TV movies and short-lived sitcoms in the 1990s. Her most prominent role in recent years has been a recurring role on *Modern Family*...a TV show.

David Caruso got the role of a lifetime when he was cast as a detective on *NYPD Blue*, a police drama that debuted in 1993 and was created by Stephen Bochco (*L.A. Law*, *Hill Street Blues*). The show was critically acclaimed, although most of that praise was for Caruso's co-star, Dennis Franz. Nevertheless, after just one season, Caruso left the show for a movie career. In 1995 two Caruso movies materialized: *Jade*, an erotic crime drama, and *Kiss of Death*, also an erotic crime drama. Both bombed at the box office. Caruso was stuck—his movies tanked so hard that he couldn't get any more roles, nor could he get TV work because in order to get off of *NYPD Blue*, he'd signed an agreement prohibiting him from working in TV until 1997. Caruso stayed unemployed until CBS hired him for the short-lived drama *Michael Hayes*. (Happy ending: He starred on *CSI: Miami* from 2002 to 2012.)

> "HIS MOVIES TANKED SO HARD THAT HE COULDN'T GET ANY MORE ROLES, NOR COULD HE GET TV WORK."

Jeff Conaway started out as a movie star—his breakthrough role was as Kenickie in 1978's *Grease*. He then moved to TV to portray Bobby, a struggling actor who works as a cabbie on *Taxi*. After three seasons, Conaway was fired from the show because of a drug problem. Conaway thought he'd restart his film career...but it didn't work out. He didn't get cast in a single movie for two years. In 1983 he returned to TV in the fantasy series *Wizards and Warriors*, which was canceled after two episodes. Conaway acted in films sporadically after that, but returned to TV in 2006... as a participant on VH1's *Celebrity Fit Club*, but he dropped out because of his drug addiction; he then sought help on VH1's *Celebrity Rehab*. Sadly, Conaway died from an assortment of health problems in 2011 at age 60.

REAL QUESTIONS FROM THE BUTTERBALL TURKEY THANKSGIVING HOTLINE

Should I remove the plastic wrap before I cook my turkey?

. . . .

The family dog is inside the turkey and can't get out.

. . . .

I need to drive two hours with my frozen turkey before I cook it. Will it stay frozen if I tie it to the luggage rack on the roof of my car?

. . . .

Does the turkey go in the oven feet first, or head first?

. . . .

Can I baste my turkey with suntan lotion?

. . . .

I scrubbed my raw turkey with a toothbrush dipped in bleach for three hours. Is that enough to kill all the harmful bacteria?

. . . .

I didn't want to cook the whole turkey, so I cut it in half with a chainsaw. How do I get the chainsaw oil out of the turkey?

. . . .

How long does it take to cook a turkey if I leave the oven door open the entire time? That was how my mom always did it.

. . . .

How do I prepare a turkey for vegetarians?

BURNING MAN

King Charles VI of France spent much of his reign struggling to maintain his sanity. He suffered from "bouts of madness," during which he became convinced he was made of glass. He also had a nasty habit of forgetting his own name and running amok through the halls of his Parisian residence. (Historians now believe he had paranoid schizophrenia.) His mental health issues contributed to bitter power struggles within the French government. But before all that there was the Bal des Ardents ("The Ball of the Burning Men").

In 1393 Charles decided to host a masquerade ball to celebrate the third wedding of a widow named Catherine de Fastaverin, one of his queen's ladies-in-waiting. The gala was scheduled for the night of January 28 at the Hotel Saint-Pol, the royal residence. Back then, the weddings of widows were cause for wild parties involving loud music, lavish costumes, and silly shenanigans. So for this occasion, Huguet de Guisay, a nobleman with a reputation for being a colossal jerk, came up with a plan to prank Catherine.

He convinced Charles and five of his knights to dress up as masked "wild men" in disguises made out of wood, resin, and weeds. The participants knew the costumes were highly flammable, so plans were made ahead of time to extinguish all the torches in the hall where the party was held. At the designated moment, the lights went out and the pranksters burst in, shouting obscenities, howling, and dancing frantically. Five of the wild men were chained together.

Everyone was having a blast until the Duke of Orléans, Charles's brother, showed up late, drunk as a skunk, and carrying a lit torch. According to one account, he held his torch over one of the chained pranksters' heads while trying to figure out the man's identity. Then a spark fell, setting his costume ablaze. Chaos ensued as the fire spread from one wild man to another. They cried out in pain as the costumes of other partygoers burst into flames. Everyone stormed the exits, running for their lives.

The king was saved by the quick intervention of the Duchess of Berry, who threw her huge skirt over his body to protect him from flying sparks. The only other prankster who survived was the Sieur de Nantouillet, who jumped into a vat of wine and hid there until the fire was extinguished. Several more attendees later succumbed to burns and other injuries. Huguet, the mastermind of the prank, died a few days later, reportedly badmouthing his fellow conspirators until his final breath.

French citizens were outraged that the king's advisers allowed him to put himself in such danger, while others saw it as a sign that the monarchy had become too self-absorbed and decadent. To quell death threats against the king's couriers and other aristocrats and offset a possible revolt over the scandal, the royal court somberly marched through the streets of Paris all the way to Notre Dame Cathedral, where they paid penance for the disastrous prank.

Orléans received most of the blame for the tragedy, and his reputation, already tarnished by earlier accusations of sorcery (yup, sorcery), never recovered. The ball is also considered by many French historians to mark the beginning of Charles's slide into madness and irrelevance. By the end of the century, his role as king had become purely ceremonial.

WRONG TURN

Truck driver Jabin Bogan, 27, made a pickup at a warehouse in El Paso, Texas, in April 2012 and set off for Phoenix, Arizona. Bogan made a wrong turn...and found himself at the Mexican border.

With no room to turn around, he crossed into Mexico, turned around just a minute or so later, and headed back to the States. When he got to the customs check-point, his truck was searched: Bogan was carrying 268,000 rounds of ammunition destined for a Phoenix gun shop. Mexican customs agents didn't believe his story—and Bogan was arrested on arms-smuggling charges.

Bogan's mother, employer, and several U.S. politicians lobbied the Mexican government on his behalf, and he was released...seven months later.

ANIMAULED

Tigered! Norman Buwalda of Southwold, Ontario, kept a 650-pound Siberian tiger as a pet, despite the objections of his neighbors. In 2004 they complained to authorities after the big cat nearly killed a 10-year-old boy. (Buwalda allowed him to go into the cage to take pictures for a school project; the camera's flash upset the tiger, who took his annoyance out on the boy.) But Buwalda, who was chairman of the Canadian Exotic Animal Owners' Association, fought tooth and claw against a proposed bylaw that would have made it illegal for him to keep exotic pets. Good news: He won! Bad news: In 2010 one of Buwalda's relatives discovered Norman Buwalda's mutilated body inside the cage with the tiger.

Roached! In October 2012, 32-year-old Edward Archbold entered a contest at a local pet store in Deerfield Beach, Florida: Whoever could eat the most live cockroaches and mealworms would win a python valued at $850! Archbold, who wanted to win the snake for a friend, wolfed down "60 grams of meal worms, 35 three-inch-long 'super worms,' and a bucket of discoid roaches." He had to cover his mouth while chewing to keep the bugs from crawling out. Good news: Archbold won! Bad news: A few minutes later, while standing in the parking lot, he started puking the bugs back up, and a few got stuck in his throat. He was rushed to the hospital, but died before he got there.

Swanned! Employed by a company that uses swans to keep geese away from golf courses and condo complexes, Anthony Hensley was sent to a pond near Des Plaines, Illinois, in April 2012 to check on the swans there. He paddled his kayak across the water to get a closer look, and a large female swan became agitated by his presence. Then, according to witnesses, the big bird rushed Hensley. Not wanting to hurt the swan (who was protecting her nest), he didn't fight back. His kayak flipped over and he fell into the water. By this time, several other swans had joined the melee—they brutally attacked Hensley as he tried to swim away. He went under and drowned.

Beed! Jaam Singh Girdhan Barela was performing a cremation ritual at his wife's funeral in India when the smoke upset a nearby beehive. The bees swarmed the funeral party and everyone fled... except Barela. He chose to stay and complete the ritual, but he wasn't able to because the bees stung him so many times that he died.

Beared! Most big-predator cages have two sections, one of which the animal can be kept in so the keeper can safely enter the other section for feeding and cleaning. Michael Walz of Ross

Township, Pennsylvania, kept his black bear in a single-section cage only 15 square feet. One day in 2009, his wife, Kelly Ann, entered the cage and threw a handful of dry dog food at the 350-pound beast to keep it occupied while she cleaned up. But the bear wasn't interested in dog food. It attacked her. A neighbor ran and got his gun and killed the bear, but not in time to save Kelly Ann. "Why this woman chose to go in the same area that the bear was in is beyond me," said Tim Conway of the Pennsylvania Game Commission.

Hippopotamussed! In 2005 Marius Els, an army major from South Africa, took in a baby hippo that had been rescued from a flooded river near his farm. Els named his new pet Humphrey and tried to domesticate it. His neighbors warned him that hippos can't be tamed, but Els ignored them and raised Humphrey "like a son." (He even liked to take rides on his "son's" back.) "There's a relationship between me and Humphrey," he told *The Guardian* in 2011, "and that's what some people don't understand." Apparently, Els didn't understand the relationship, either. Later that year, when Humphrey was six (and Els was 40), the one-ton beast's savage side erupted: "Humphrey-Humphrey Hippo" bit Els repeatedly with his giant canines and then dragged his limp body into the same river from which the animal had been rescued...and drowned him.

TERRIBLE, TERRIBLE TYPOS

I n 1987 Kamjai Thavorn was sentenced to 20 years in an Indonesian prison for heroin posses- sion. In 2007 Thavorn told the warden that his sentence had ended and he should be set free. But according to prison paperwork, Thavorn began serving in *1997*—not 1987—and still had a decade left to go. For the next three years, he pleaded to be set free...to no avail. He might still be behind bars today if not for a chance meeting in 2010 with Indonesia's justice minister, who was touring the facility. Thavorn told the minister his situa- tion, the matter was looked into, and Thavorn was finally freed.

• In late 2007, two Maryland state assessment workers, both new to the job, were entering data into all of the counties' proposed budgets for 2008. At one point, one of them accidentally entered the estimated taxable real estate for Montgomery County in 2008 values, instead of the actual 2007 numbers. That single incorrect num- ber created a domino effect that threw off several other county budget estimates. Once officials real- ized something was wrong, it took eight months and a small army of number-crunchers to find the error. In all, it threw off budget estimates by $16 billion and cost taxpayers more than $31 million to correct.

STRIPPER ACCIDENTS

BOMBS AWAY!
In November 2010, Patrick Gallagher's friends bought him a "bachelor package" at the Penthouse Club, a Philadelphia strip joint, for his bachelor party. As part of the package he was invited onstage with the dancers, who made him lie down next to the stripper pole. That's when a stripper climbed high up on the pole, slid down, landed on Gallagher—and ruptured his bladder. "From a great height, she launched herself down onto his abdomen," his attorney, Neil T. Murray, told reporters. Gallagher needed surgery, and he sued the Penthouse Club for $50,000 for medical costs as well as "pain, humiliation, and mental anguish."

DO NOT TOUCH, DO NOT LOOK

Like Mr. Gallagher in the item above, Michael Ireland was celebrating his bachelor party at a strip joint, this one the Cheetah in West Palm Beach, Florida, in September 2008. At one point during the festivities, he was watching dancer Sakeena Shageer perform atop the club's bar. Shageer wasn't paying much attention to where she was gyrating, and one of her stiletto heels ended up in one of Ireland's eye sockets. He suffered a broken

orbital bone, a broken nose, and possibly perma-
nently impaired vision. He sued the club, and the
Cheetah eventually settled the case for $650,000.
However, Shageer's take on the story is a little
different. She claims that while she was dancing
with her back turned to Ireland, he spanked her,
hard. As the club has a strict "no touching" policy,
Shageer says that she instantly and instinctively
reacted by kicking out her foot. "I didn't mean to
mess up his face like that," she said.

STRIPPER WAR

In October 2012, two strippers got into a fight
at Hot Bodies, an Austin, Texas, strip club. Then
another joined in...and yet another...and BAM!—it
was a full-on bench-clearing stripper brawl. In the
middle of the melee, stripper Victoria Perez took
off one of her high-heeled shoes and winged it
across the room. In a repeat of the Michael Ireland
story almost too exact to be true, the heel of that
shoe went right into an eye socket of an unidentified Hot Bodies patron. When police arrived
minutes later, they found 17 strippers in a full-tilt
rumble—and the unidentified man wailing and
holding his hands over his bloody face. He was
taken to the hospital and, fortunately, released
that night—but doctors said the man might eventually lose his eye. Perez, who police officers said
was caught on security footage throwing the shoe,
told them it "may have been" her who did it. She
was arrested on a charge of aggravated assault
with a deadly weapon—the high-heeled shoe—and
jailed on $50,000 bail.

FROM COPPING A FEEL TO COPPING A PLEA

In July 2012, Wendy Haddon of Humpty Doo, Australia (really), was treated by her friends to a "hen's night," the Australian equivalent of a bachelorette party, at

"BUT THEY WEREN'T STRIPPERS DRESSED LIKE COPS—THEY WERE ACTUAL COPS."

the Humpty Doo Hotel's bar. Hours into the party, two carloads of men in police uniforms pulled into the parking lot, and the drunken gals ran outside shouting, "Here come the strippers! Here come the strippers!" But they weren't strippers dressed like cops—they were actual cops. Senior Sergeant Louise Jorgensen told reporters the next day, "Someone approached the officers about taking their clothes off. They weren't willing to do that." She added that the two officers "nearly had their shirts taken off, but they managed to escape with their dignity intact." Bride-to-be Haddon spoke to reporters, too, saying, "We thought they were going to be strippers. But, no, they weren't. Bugger."

The cops actually took the mistake in fun, and even posed for pictures with Haddon. One of the photos showed an officer pretending to arrest Haddon—standing behind her as he bent her over the hood of his police car.

GREAT BUTTS OF FIRE

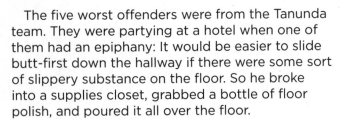

Do right by yourself, your teammates, and your club." That was the friendly advice the Barossa, South Australia, police department posted on its Facebook page ahead of the annual end-of-season celebrations for Australian rules football teams. Many players failed to heed that advice.

The five worst offenders were from the Tanunda team. They were partying at a hotel when one of them had an epiphany: It would be easier to slide butt-first down the hallway if there were some sort of slippery substance on the floor. So he broke into a supplies closet, grabbed a bottle of floor polish, and poured it all over the floor.

Then they all slid down the hallway. Whee!

Then their buttocks all started burning. Badly. The footballers started screaming as they tried to wipe off their rears, but that just made it worse. It turned out that the inebriated footballer had unwittingly snatched an industrial cleaner chock-full of hazardous acid-based chemicals that burn skin on contact. Ouch.

CORPORATE GAFFES

Bloody informative. British Aircraft Corporation made an in-house training film in 1976 to instruct its factory workers on the importance of wearing protective goggles. However, the film was of the "if you don't do this, this will happen variety," meaning it included graphic depictions of on-the-job eye gougings, losses, and injuries. One worker fainted as he fell off his chair, opening a gash in his head that required stitches.

What a card! In 1938, about two years after Social Security debuted, a wallet manufacturer in Lockport, New York, put mock Social Security cards in its wallets (similar to the fake pictures used today). But the company didn't put a fake number on them—they used 078-05-1120, the number of the company's secretary. It was half the size of an actual Social Security card and stamped "specimen" in red ink, but hundreds of people still assumed for some reason that it was a real card, *their* card, and that that was their number. It wasn't fully straightened out until the 1970s.

Yo quiero basura! Taco Bell's most famous ad campaign involved a talking Chihuahua going up to people on the street and saying, "Yo quiero Taco Bell." It was

the '90s most famous fast food catchphrase, the "Where's the beef?" of its time. The ad campaign lasted from 1997 to 2000, when it was yanked off the air after Taco Bell discovered that its sales had actually *dropped* by 6 percent since the introduction of the Spanish-speaking dog mascot. Some fast-food industry analysts think it's because people don't want to see themselves as the kind of people who eat what dogs eat: Dogs eat literally anything, including garbage. Even worse: In 2003 two men sued Taco Bell, claiming they had pitched a "talking Chihuahua ad campaign" six years earlier, and that Taco Bell rejected it, but then ran it anyway without paying the men anything. The advertisers won the suit, and Taco Bell had to pay them $42 million.

D'oh! In 1993 the U.S. Postal Service released its most popular commemorative postage stamp ever: the one featuring a young Elvis Presley (which won out over an older Elvis in a national poll). The USPS sold out its run of 517 million of the 29-cent stamps. In 2009, to commemorate the 20th anniversary of *The Simpsons* debut on Fox, the Postal Service debuted a line of five Simpsons stamps, one for each member of the Simpson nuclear family. The agency printed a staggering one billion 44-cent Simpsons stamps in all, twice that of the Elvis run. How many did they ultimately sell? Not even as many as Elvis. Only 318 million stamps were sold. In 2012 the USPS raised the rate (and standard stamp value) to 45 cents, rendering the 682 million unsold Simpsons stamps in need of an additional one-cent stamp to mail a letter. The USPS pulped them, a waste of $1.2 million in printing costs, not to mention the $286 million retail value of the unsold postage. This debacle is just a drop in the bucket for the USPS's woes: It lost $15 billion in fiscal 2012 and was even considering dropping national Saturday mail delivery. Overall, fewer people are using first-class stamps to mail letters, opting instead for email and other forms of electronic communication—especially young people, the target demographic for the Simpsons stamps.

Royally dumb. Legend has it that in 1934 Cunard Cruise Line planned to name its gigantic new flagship ocean liner the *Queen Victoria*, after the deceased British monarch. The company thought it might be a good idea to seek approval from the current monarch, King George V. Cunard director Thomas Royden asked King George for his blessing to name the ship "after the greatest queen this country has ever known." The king replied, "That is the greatest compliment ever paid to my wife. I'll ask her." And so, the *Queen Mary* was named.

TEXT MESSAGING ACCIDENTS

Hey, I don't think this is working. I'm breaking up with you.

I'm your wife. You can't exactly break up with me. I'm living in your house. You could just walk over to the other side of the room and tell me you want to get divorced.

Oops, sorry. That was meant for someone else.

Oh ok ☺ Wait...WHAT?

....

How's our pregnant little daughter?

Mom! How did you know that?

I meant precious. Sorry, typo. WAIT, WHAT?

....

Your mom and I are going to divorce next month.

What? Why! Call me please?

I wrote Disney and this phone changed it. We are going to Disney.

....

Where is Granny? I thought she was going to be here for Thanksgiving?

Grandma is in the grave.

What grave? What are you saying?

Oops, sorry. Garage.

....

Do I look like a cow?

Moo

☹ Great

Moo

Be nice! That's mean

That was the worst autocorrect ever. I said Nooooo, I swear to God.

"HEY, Y'ALL—WATCH THIS!"

Roamin' Roman. Roman Retynski often described himself as invincible. He was not. Trying to channel his inner Indiana Jones one night, the 34-year-old Alaskan was driving his pickup truck at 60 mph on a bumpy rural road. "Grab the wheel!" he shouted to his girlfriend. Then he was out the window and onto the hood and gone. The next day, Retynski's friends told reporters they were sad the avid car surfer was dead, but not all that surprised.

Le manteau de la mort. On a freezing February morning in Paris in 1912, a crowd gathered at the Eiffel Tower to watch Austrian tailor Franz Reichelt test his new invention: an overcoat with a built-in parachute. He'd received permission to perform the test—on the condition that he use a dummy. When Reichelt arrived, he announced that *he* would be the dummy. Onlookers tried to dissuade the "Flying Tailor" (as he called himself), but Reichelt was adamant. He carried his bulky contraption up to a platform nearly 200 feet above the ground, stepped up onto a chair next to the railing, peered out over the edge, and stood there. He looked down again, and stood there some more. And then some more. Finally, Reichelt took a deep breath (his last) and stepped off. His parachute did not open, and he slammed face-first into the rock-hard ground at 130 feet per second. He left a crater nearly six inches deep.

BMW DOA. A century later in Germany, some adventurous young men were filming a *Jackass*-like web series called *Bavarian Dumbasses*. A 20-year-old daredevil named Tobias tied one end of a rope to a playground merry-go-round and the other end to a BMW. His friends then duct-taped him to the outer railing of the merry-go-round. Tobias gave the signal, and his buddy floored the BMW, sending the merry-go-round spinning at breakneck speed...which is exactly what happened to Tobias. The duct tape was no match for the centrifugal force, and the stuntman was flung into the air. He hit the ground so hard that his neck broke and his skull cracked open. Not only did Tobias succumb to his injuries, but the merry-go-round was later removed from the playground.

Lion in wait. In 2006 Ohtaj Humbat Ohli Makhmudov, 45, set out to prove that God exists. He went to the lions' den at the Kiev Zoo in Ukraine, used a rope to tie himself to a railing, and climbed in. As onlookers yelled at him to get out of there, Makhmudov walked in between four lions and announced, "Because God loves me, the lions will not harm me!" An atheist lioness named Veronica pounced on him and nearly bit his head off. He died instantly.

Drawing a blank. Jon-Erik Hexum was an up-and-coming actor until he got bored one day in 1984.

During a halt in filming his spy series, *Cover-Up*, Hexum started messing around with a .44 Magnum that his character was going to load with blanks. Blanks aren't bullets, Hexum surmised, so the gun couldn't hurt him. But blanks consist of gunpowder (which explodes) behind a wad of paper (which keeps the powder in the chamber). So a gun loaded with blanks not only fires, it also has a severe kickback. Not knowing that, Hexum placed the barrel on his temple and then said to the cast and crew, "Let's see if I get myself with this one." The bad news: Hexum got himself. The good news: A dying man got his heart; an elderly blind man got one of his corneas; a blind little girl got his other cornea; an ailing grandma got one of his kidneys; a dying five-year-old boy got his other kidney; and a severely burned toddler got some of Hexum's skin.

Go Vikings! Of course, the ultimate way to show off is to carry around the severed head of your slain enemy. After a ninth-century battle, Sigurd the Mighty, the Viking Earl of Orkney, defeated his greatest foe, Máel Brigte. He carried the dead man's head as he rode home on his horse, eager to show the gruesome trophy off to his people. But during the ride home, one of Brigte's teeth gouged a hole in Sigurd's leg. With antiseptic cream still a millennium away, Sigurd's wound became infected and he died a slow, painful death.

THE STONER REPORT

Burning question. Robert Michelson of Farmington, Connecticut, called 911 one day in February 2011. When the dispatcher asked if there was a crime in progress, Michelson said, "Possibly. I was just growing some marijuana and was just wondering how much trouble you can get in for one plant." After a long pause, the dispatcher replied, "It depends on how big the plant is." "It's only a seedling," said Michelson. The dispatcher informed him that having a plant *does* constitute possession of marijuana. Michelson thanked her and hung up. The dispatcher alerted the police, who arrived at Michelson's house a short time later. However, there was no plant. Michelson told police he was only thinking about growing marijuana. However, he was still arrested, as he was in possession of marijuana, marijuana seeds, and several bongs.

Must-stash. In February 2011, Joel Dobrin, 32, of San Diego, California, was driving down a road in Sherman County, Oregon. Some marijuana and hashish rode shotgun on the front seat of his pickup truck. He was pulled over by a sheriff's deputy, but before the cop could get to his window, Dobrin grabbed a sock that was lying on the floor of the truck and stashed his drugs inside it. But his dog, a pit bull, grabbed the sock and started playing tug-of-war with it, and the sock flew out the open window of the truck. The sheriff simply retrieved the sock and found the drugs. "I wish everyone traveled with their own personal drug dog," a sheriff's spokesman told reporters.

Green giant. Ramiro Gonzalez, 30, of Progreso, Texas, was driving a tractor-trailer filled with papayas in the far south of the state one day in January 2011. A sheriff's deputy pulled the truck over and found 3,103 pounds of marijuana underneath the papayas. Gonzalez was arrested on felony drug trafficking charges. He probably would have gotten away with it, too, if it hadn't been for the expired tags on his truck, which was the only reason he'd been stopped in the first place.

Above the law. Robert Watson was driving down an East Haven, Connecticut, road late one night in April 2011. Watson came across a police sobriety checkpoint—where police found marijuana in his car. (He had also been drinking, but was just under the legal limit.) Watson was arrested for possession of marijuana. A blood test found that he also had small amounts of cocaine in his system. Unfortunately, Watson was a member of the Rhode Island House of Representatives—and had a record of stridently opposing marijuana legalization, and of voting for stiff penalties for drug offenses. As of press time, Watson had pleaded not guilty to all charges.

BABY ON BOARD

In May 2012, a video appeared on YouTube showing closed-circuit tape of the inside of a laundromat. A couple and a small boy can be seen at a machine not far from the camera. The man picks the boy up off the floor and sticks him in a large front-loading washing machine. He closes the door, steps back, and looks at the child in what seems like a harmless game.

Then the machine automatically starts spinning. And filling with water. The man and woman rush to the machine—but they can't open the door: It automatically locked when the machine started. The couple frantically try to get the door open, run to get help, and try again to open the door as a crowd grows around the machine. Finally a man runs up, throws some tables out of the way, opens a hatch behind the machine, reaches into it—and the machine stops running. The door finally opens and the boy is taken out. Luckily, the boy was fine—he only got a few bruises.

But, weirdly, if it hadn't been for the video being posted on YouTube, the child's mother might never have known about the incident. The laundromat was quickly identified by YouTube viewers as the Federal Laundromat in Camden, New Jersey. A news station there played the video, and the child's mother, Sakia David, saw it—and saw her one-year-old son Saimeir being put into a washing machine by a man she didn't know.

The woman in the video? She was the boy's babysitter. And when she'd brought him home with bruises that day, she told Sakia that Saimeir had fallen down some stairs. Camden police investigated the incident and said that nothing criminal had occurred—the man was simply playing "peek-a-boo" with the boy—and said the man and woman in the video would not be facing charges.

SPOILER ALERT!

O n the day it was set to air the seventh-season finale of *Top Chef*, Bravo posted on its website a clip featuring a reunion of that season's contestants. It was meant to go up after the show, however, as the clip opens with host Andy Cohen saying, "Before we get into anything, we have to congratulate the winner of *Top Chef: D.C.*, Kevin." Bravo pulled the video a few hours later, but it was too late, and the season-ruining scoop had already spread around the Internet.

• In 2011, the second season of AMC's zombie drama *The Walking Dead* featured a shocking twist in its second-to-last episode. (Shane, Sheriff Grimes's best friend and an increasingly loose cannon, attempts to kill Grimes and take control over the group of survivors, forcing Grimes to kill Shane, who becomes a zombie soon thereafter and is then killed.) The show sells a ton of DVD sets, so AMC was already taking orders for Season 2 before the season was done airing. The fate of Shane had not yet been aired when *The Walking Dead* ad on AMC's site appeared, listing special features such as a look at "Shane's last episode."

"THE SEASON-RUINING SCOOP HAD ALREADY SPREAD AROUND THE INTERNET."

FOR WHOM THE BELL TOLLS

Not so long ago, the telegraph (a coded message of electrical pulses over a charged wire) was the dominant and only quick form of telecommunication. More than 50 different telegraph companies were operating within the U.S. by 1851, the year the New York and Mississippi Valley Printing Telegraph Company was founded. A decade later, only a handful were left, among them the New York and Mississippi company under its new name, Western Union Telegraph Company.

In the 1870s, another major telecommunications innovation occurred: Alexander Graham Bell drew up plans for a new technology he called a "harmonic telegraph," and his company, the Volta Laboratory, began filing patents. As the idea evolved, Bell began to consider a device that could transmit the human voice, though he couldn't figure out how he would pull off such a feat. Luckily for Bell, patent law at the time allowed him to file for an invention for which there was not yet a working model. So Bell received a patent for the "telephone," which he technically hadn't invented yet. And he was granted it just before a competitor, Elisha Gray, filed his own notice of invention for a telephone.

On March 10, 1876, he succeeded in transmitting speech, one week after his patent had been granted. Unfortunately, he used a technology described not in his application, but in Gray's. Seeing the long legal battles ahead, and fearing for the future of an invention that still wasn't complete, Bell offered to sell the telephone patents to Western Union—a company that at the time was worth tens of millions of dollars—for $100,000. A Western Union memo shows the logic of Western Union as it turned down Bell:

> The Telephone purports to transmit the speaking voice over telegraph wires. We found that the voice is very weak and indistinct, and grows even weaker when long wires are used between the transmitter and receiver. Technically, we do not see that this device will be ever capable of sending recognizable speech over a distance of several miles. This device is inherently of no use to us. We do not recommend its purchase.

It wasn't long before telegraphs were being removed from locations all over the country to make way for telephones. Western Union wasn't immediately destroyed by the loss of the opportunity to rule the world's communications systems. It continued in business, offering the first charge card for consumers in 1914, as well as the first candygrams in the 1960s, and even satellites in the 1970s. But mounting debts and falling profits led the company to begin divesting its telecommunications-based assets starting in the 1980s. In February 2006, the company announced the end of its telegram services.

THESE STORIES SUCK

Daniel Blackner is a performance artist. He's also a little person, and he is best known as playing "Captain Dan the Demon Dwarf" in a show called Circus of Horrors at the annual Edinburgh Fringe Festival of bizarre and avant-garde performances. During his 2007 performance, Blackner brought a vacuum cleaner onto the stage...attached to his penis. But the safe adhesive connecting man to machine came loose, so, thinking quickly, Blackner affixed the vacuum to his genitals with extra-strong glue. He got stuck. He was taken to a hospital, where it took nurses an hour to free him.

• In 2008 a building contractor from Poland (unnamed in reports) was working in a hospital when he decided he needed to clean his underpants. So he went into the empty hospital cafeteria, lowered his pants, and went about cleaning his underwear... with a vacuum cleaner. A security guard caught him in the act with the cleaning machine, which was a "Henry Hoover," a vacuum with a huge, smiling face painted on its front and a hose for a nose. The contractor was asked to leave the premises immediately (and to leave the vacuum).

SHREDS UP!

A Manhattan lawyer named Saul Finkelstein made an unsettling discovery during New York City's 2012 Macy's Thanksgiving Day Parade: Some of the pieces of confetti had decipherable words and numbers on them—the full names, dates of birth, Social Security numbers, and banking information of detectives from the Nassau County Police Department (NCPD), which serves nearby Long Island. Finkelstein even found strips of paper with legible details about presidential candidate Mitt Romney's motorcade (which had been on Long Island a month earlier). Finkelstein and his son brought several handfuls of the confetti home and alerted the NCPD, who sent over an officer to take it away. The police promised to investigate the matter.

But what's to investigate? There are two ways to put documents into a shredder: the long way and the short way. Do it the long way, and the shredder shreds the paper perpendicular to the text lines, thus cutting it up into little, illegible pieces. But if the documents are loaded into the shredder the other way, the cuts are parallel, leading to entire lines of text being readable.

Even more curious: How did Macy's, the department store that runs the parade, obtain the sensitive confetti from a police department in another city? A Macy's spokesperson said they didn't—they use only "commercially manufactured, multi-colored confetti, not shredded, homemade, or printed paper of any kind." But spectators often "bring their own confetti." So that means someone who works at the NCPD had brought bagfuls of improperly shredded documents to America's most popular parade. An internal investigation soon revealed the two officers who had brought the shreds, and they were reprimanded.

THE CAMERA IS ON

In October 2009, Australian ABC2 news anchor Virginia Trioli was in the middle of a program when she cut to an interview she had taped earlier with an Australian politician, Barnaby Joyce. While the segment played Trioli joked with someone in the studio, making a face, along with the universally understood circle movement of a finger at the side of her head—implying that Mr. Joyce was "crazy." And...the camera cut away from the segment and back to her just as she was making the gestures. Trioli abruptly stopped what she doing, went back to her serious news face, and continued the broadcast. Trioli was forced to make a shamefaced on-air apology to viewers the next day.

THE PUNKIEST OF PUNKS

Stiv Bators was a major star in the late '70s punk rock scene as the front man of the Dead Boys. After playing a murderous juvenile delinquent in John Waters's cult comedy *Polyester*, Bators went to England to form the goth rock band the Lords of the New Church. Bators's stage antics were brutal. He often stuck his head inside the bass drum during loud jams. One time, he banged his head on an amplifier so hard he cracked his skull. (After receiving a few stitches, he was back onstage for the second set.) Another time, Bators tossed his microphone cord over a rafter above the stage, wrapped it around his neck, and started pulling himself up. Some of the crowd members then "helped" him by pulling on the cord even more. Seeing the look of panic in Bators's eyes, his bandmates quickly freed him, but he wasn't breathing. Paramedics actually pronounced him dead before they were able to revive him.

None of those antics killed Bators, but they increased his pain threshold so much that he literally didn't feel much pain as the years went on. That's why in 1990, while in Paris to record new music, Bators didn't think he needed any medical attention when he got hit by a taxi while crossing the street. After leaving the hospital because it was "too busy," he walked four miles in the rain to meet his girlfriend at their hotel room. He told her about the accident, but said he felt fine. Later that night he had trouble breathing, so his girlfriend called an ambulance. He was dead before it arrived.

It turned out that Bators had suffered a concussion and severe internal injuries from the accident. Had he been in more pain, he might have allowed the doctors to treat him, and he may have survived.

THREE DUMB DOCTORS

• John Hunter was a preeminent research scientist in the 18th century. He injected himself with several different diseases to study their effects. That's how, in 1793, he discovered that syphilis is fatal.

• A smallpox epidemic struck France in 1715 and spared no one, not even the royal family. At their palace in Versailles, court doctor Guy Fagon prescribed purges, emetics, and bleeding. Within two weeks, the entire royal family was dead. All except for Louis XV, a baby, who was spared because his nurse didn't trust Fagon and kept him hidden.

• Harold Senby of Leeds, England, visited his doctor in 1978 to check on his hearing loss. His hearing instantly improved when the doctor removed his hearing aid—it had been made for his left ear, but installed in his right. In 1958.

MEET YOUR NEW FAKE PRESIDENT

I n preparation for a victory in the 2012 presidential election, the Mitt Romney campaign created the Office of the President-Elect website to provide information about Romney's administration.

Either the campaign assumed it had the election in the bag, or it was set to go live on Election Night and nobody told it not to, but the site went live on Election Night 2012, just moments after major news outlets had called the election...for President Barack Obama. The Romney team pulled the site down in minutes, but several bloggers had already visited the site and saved screenshots. Among the highlights of the website from an alternate universe in which Romney won:

- Romney's welcome message: "I'm excited about our prospects as a nation. My priority is putting people back to work in America." Next to it was an image of a solemn Romney superimposed over an American flag.

- Details about "The Inauguration: January 21, 2013, in Washington, D.C."

- How to apply for a job in the new administration.

BIZARRE BASEBALL INJURIES

Mickey Tettleton went on the disabled list for athlete's foot, which he got from habitually tying his shoes too tight.

Rickey Henderson missed several games because of frostbite—he fell asleep on an ice pack.

Pitcher John Smoltz once burned his chest. He'd ironed a shirt... while still wearing it.

Marty Cordova went on the injured list after burning his face in a tanning bed.

Outfielder Terry Harper once high-fived a team-mate. The act separated his shoulder.

Pitcher Clarence Blethen took out his false teeth during a game and put them in his back pocket. Later, while he was sliding into second base, the teeth clamped down and bit him on the butt.

During the 1985 National League Championship Series, St. Louis Cardinals outfielder Vince Coleman was fooling around on the field and managed to get rolled up inside the stadium's tarp-rolling machine.

THE ROADSIDE BACHELOR PARTY

In June 2001, a group of guys threw a weekend-long bachelor party for a friend in Wiltshire, England. Early on Sunday afternoon, a bunch of the men grabbed the groom and his best man—the whole lot of them drunk—stuffed them into a car, drove them several miles down a major highway until they got to a very rural area, pulled over, dragged the men out of the car, and stripped them both naked.

They then covered the men with raw eggs, tomato sauce, and flour—and handcuffed their hands together. Then they drove off. Startled motorists called police some time later, when they saw the handcuffed accidental streakers stumbling along the side of the highway, coated in what looked like powdered vomit. After several hours the men were finally rescued—but not before they'd both gotten serious cases of sunburn on what was an uncharacteristically hot day. "They were very red," a police officer said. "Some bits were redder than others...if you know what I mean." Police got the men cleaned up, gave them paper gowns (like hospital gowns), and took them home. They said they would not be identifying the men...to spare them any further embarrassment.

MILD ANIMALS

Ah! **"Coyote"**! In spring 2009, a jogger in Sarnia, Ontario, got spooked when she encountered a coyote. She ran to a nearby construction site and told a worker that the coyote had barked at her, and that it looked like it was going to chase her. The construction worker called police, who found the coyote, surrounded it, and put the animal out of commission. It was quite easy—it was a cardboard, photo-realistic cutout of a coyote. Sarnia had not been aware that Sudbury, Ontario—a city 250 miles away—had installed the $30 cardboard coyote to scare away geese that were pooping all over a park. The coyote had worked well...until somebody stole it and dumped it in Sarnia.

Ah! "Alligator"! Responding to a call of an alligator threatening kids in an Independence, Missouri, neighborhood in May 2011, police officers located the creature in a yard belonging to Rick Sheridan. They fired two rounds into the animal. That's when Sheridan came running outside, yelling, "What are you doing? It's made of concrete!" When asked why he had a concrete alligator in his yard, Sheridan explained that it works better than a "No Trespassing" sign, or at least it usually does.

FAILED GOVERNMENT

Fire bad. New Mexico fire officials started a prescribed burn in May 2000 on Cerro Grande Mountain, not far from the town of Los Alamos, intending to clear out underbrush in order to make the area more resistant to forest fires. The high winds and drought conditions should have given officials a clue that maybe it wasn't the best time, but they were concerned that a worse fire might break out if they didn't. But it quickly got out of control. The Cerro Grande Fire lasted four months, burned through 48,000 acres, and destroyed 235 homes in Los Alamos. Total cost of the disaster: $1 billion.

Mind the gap. New York City Metropolitan Transit Authority officials were left red-faced in January 2009 when the opening of a new subway station had to be postponed. Reason: The gap between the platform and the train car was four inches wide. Although that distance wouldn't pose a danger to most people, it violated the Americans with Disabilities Act, which specifies that the gap can be no larger than three inches. The goof was blamed on the engineers, who had failed to take into account the slight curve of the platform. Cost of the extra inch: a two-month delay in opening the station and $200,000 to extend the platform.

LOVE HURTS

LOVE AND DEATH

A man and woman were visiting the grave of one of the woman's relatives in Ahavath Israel Cemetery in Hamilton, New Jersey, in May 2011. Things took an amorous turn (as they do in cemeteries), and the two ended up engaging in what police called "extracurricular activities" up against a headstone. Not sexy: The headstone fell on the woman's leg and broke it. Her partner called 911, and the woman was rushed to a hospital. Police investigated the matter and decided to not press charges against—or publicly identify—the duo.

LOVE TAKES WORK

In November 2007, an Australian woman was on a business trip in a rural Australian town, and one night while there she met up with a friend for dinner. Afterward, they went back to her hotel room, where they had sex. While having what was apparently quite a rambunctious time, a glass light fixture was knocked off the wall above the bed—and landed on the woman's face and broke. She required treatment for facial lacerations at a local hospital. The case made international news because the woman filed for worker's compensation for her out-of-town, after-hours, sex-related injury—and got it. Comcare, Australia's worker's compensation organization, initially refused the woman's claim, but in April 2012, after more than four years of legal wrangling, a federal judge ordered them to pay. "If the applicant had been injured while playing a game of cards in her motel room, she would be entitled to compensation," the judge said, and ruled it was the same for any other "legal recreational activity."

LOVE ON THE SILVER SCREEN

An Egyptian man identified only as "Ramadan" visited an Internet café in April 2012 and watched some porn videos. One of them, he noticed, starred his wife. He ran home, and his wife angrily denied the scurrilous accusation...and then confessed when the man showed her the proof. (He had found her in no fewer than 11 different homemade porn videos, Egyptian newspapers reported.) The woman went on to tell her husband that she had never loved him (they had four children together) and that she had been having an affair with (and filming sex acts with) a boyfriend (whom she had known before her marriage) for years. At last report, the husband said he wasn't sure if he'd be asking for a divorce. Bonus: The man told reporters that it was the very first time he had ever watched porn in his life. And that he'd only done it because he was "curious."

LOVE AND PROTECTION

A Romanian couple with five children decided in September 2004 that they didn't want to have any more kids—but they wanted to keep having sex. They decided that the husband, 43-year-old

Nicolae Popovici, would start using condoms. Popovici secured his first prophylactic with Super Glue. When he was later unable to remove it, he went to a hospital where doctors spent several hours removing the condom. The couple told doctors that part of the reason they had glued the condom on was because it was a bit "roomy," and the glue had helped it stay on. A nurse who had treated the man added that Mr. Popovici "thought the condom could be used several times, and he wanted it stuck on his penis so he could use it again later."

LOVE ON THE RUN

One night in September 2012, Amanda Linscott engaged in sexual activity with a man she had met at a bar in Port Charlotte, Florida. The man was driving a car while said activity was occurring. Sometime during the encounter, Linscott demanded that the man give her money. The man said he didn't have any, so Linscott pulled a revolver out of her purse and pressed it to the man's head. The man grabbed the gun, punched Linscott, the two fought, the car careened into a palm tree, went airborne, and plowed through two yards before finally coming to a halt. Linscott jumped from the car and fled, but was arrested a short time later. She was charged with armed robbery. The man was not charged with a crime.

YES, VIRGINIA...

The Elf on the Shelf is a gift-shop staple and a modern-day Christmas tradition. Parents buy their kids a Santa's elf doll and name it, thus imbuing it with magical powers. It then sits somewhere in the home and serves as Santa's eyes and ears in the weeks leading up to Christmas, supposedly giving a report to the Man in Red each night before moving to a new perch in the child's home. One big rule: Kids are not allowed to touch the elves, as it drains them of their elfin magic...and reflects poorly on the children when Santa is making his naughty-or-nice list.

However, as you probably know, Santa Claus isn't real, and the Elf on the Shelf doesn't really have magical spying capabilities. But it's a vital part of the delightful Santa tradition in millions of American homes. In December 2012, *Good Morning America* ran a segment on the Elf on the Shelf phenomenon. It included video of parents talking about how they hide their elf, along with video of parents moving the elf. Reporter Lara Spencer even manhandled one, robbing the elf of his magic! Spencer had to apologize on the air after hundreds of parents complained to *GMA* that their kids had seen the report and figured out the truth. Spencer backpedaled, claiming the elf she touched hadn't been named yet, and so was safe.

SKYFALLS

DIE ANOTHER DAY
"It was terrifying!" said Fearless Felix, negating his own nickname. To be fair, he did spend four and a half terrifying minutes hurtling toward earth while caught in a "death spin." Fearless Felix is Felix Baumgartner, 43, an Austrian "supersonic skydiver." In 2012 he attempted to become the only human being to ever break the sound barrier without the aid of a vehicle. He ascended to the stratosphere 24 miles above Roswell, New Mexico, in a helium balloon made just for the stunt. Then—wearing a 100-pound insulated, pressurized suit—he jumped out (from a world-record highest altitude) and assumed an arrowlike "delta position" to gain momentum. "The exit was perfect," he said, "but then I started tumbling. I really picked up speed, it got very brutal." Amazingly, Baumgartner maintained consciousness while spinning at 830 mph in thin, subfreezing air. He finally got out of the spin at about 5,000 feet, but when he opened his parachute, his hand got stuck in the cord. After he freed his hand, he looked up to see that the strings had twisted around the main parachute. Luckily, the chute untangled just in time to not kill him. Afterward, Baumgartner became engaged to his girlfriend and he promised to take up a safer hobby—piloting rescue helicopters.

YOU ONLY LIVE TWICE

Two skydivers whose combined ages were 135 met their end in tandem. The older of the two, 75-year-old Claudette Porter, had listed skydiving as one of her bucket-list items. So in 2011, her granddaughter, Anna Vera, set up the jump in Mesquite, Nevada, as a birthday present. Porter's instructor, James Fonnesbeck, 60, had more than 11,000 successful jumps to his name (including one as a skydiving Elvis in the 1991 film *Honeymoon in Vegas*). Vera was jumping, too, also in tandem with an instructor. Up in the plane, Porter smiled at her granddaughter and then jumped out. Vera and her instructor followed. Everything went fine for the younger pair, but Vera watched in horror as something went horribly wrong with her grandma's jump. Neither of the chutes opened properly and the pair spun toward the ground. Vera screamed. Her tandem instructor just kept repeating, "Don't look." Neither skydiver survived.

LIVE AND LET DIE

Englishman Liam Byrne's first jump nearly became the last thing he ever did. But luckily he missed a church (barely) and landed next to it...30 feet up in a tree. Then he hung there for 45 minutes until firefighters could get him down. Despite six hours of training, "he was supposed to be in an arched position when he jumped so that he moved away from the deploying parachute." But Byrne, who said he was "nervous," flailed when he exited the plane, and the chute became tangled in his arm. "What do I do?" he yelled into his radio. "Deploy your backup chute!" the instructor yelled back. So he did, but then the backup chute became tangled in the primary chute, and he went into a spin. Thankfully, the big tree saved Byrne's life. He walked away with only a few scratches and bruises. "I normally don't like heights," he said—and he probably still doesn't.

* * * * *

November 22, 1963, is a dark day in history—that's the day President John F. Kennedy was gunned down in Dallas, Texas. A few hours later, Vice President Lyndon B. Johnson was sworn in as president. But Johnson almost died an untimely death that day, too. At his residence in Washington, D.C., that night, his private Secret Service detail, Gerald Blaine, was routinely patrolling the premises. On high alert due to the Kennedy assassination, Blaine saw a dark figure coming out of the house. Blaine pointed his semiautomatic gun at the man, and put his finger on the trigger. That's when he realized he was holding a gun— and had nearly shot—President Johnson. Johnson, Blaine later recounted, didn't say a word, and went right back inside.

OOPS!

PLASTIC SURGERY DISASTERS

Michael Jackson was once the poster child for extensive plastic surgeries rendering a person nightmarishly unrecognizable, but he can't hold a candle to Jocelyn Wildenstein. She's a New York socialite who went under the knife numerous times in order to look more like an exotic cat.

Born into a middle-class family in Switzerland in 1940, Jocelyn Périsset started dating a movie producer at age 17 and joined the jetset, living in Paris and globetrotting in style. While on safari in Kenya in 1977, she met Alec Wildenstein, a French billionaire. Jocelyn, a skilled hunter, helped him track down a lion that was causing trouble on his family's ranch. They got married in Las Vegas in 1978.

The Wildensteins continued to share a passion for big cats—they kept two tigers as pets in a "bulletproof glass cave" at the ranch. After a year of marriage, the two decided to visit a clinic for "his-and-hers eyelifts." This is when Jocelyn developed an unhealthy desire to endlessly improve herself. Friends claim that Alec preferred women who were youthful and catlike, and that

"SHE TOOK ON AN APPEARANCE SOMEWHERE BETWEEN AN ALIEN AND A FELINE."

Jocelyn was eager—perhaps too eager—to please him as she grew older. Over the 1980s and 1990s, she underwent so many plastic surgeries that she took on an appearance somewhere between an alien and a feline.

Upon seeing his wife's face after a series of drastic procedures, Alec supposedly screamed in horror, which only encouraged her to return to her surgeon for even more tweaks. He later told a reporter "she seems to think that you fix a face the same way you fix a house." Total cost of the surgeries: reportedly in excess of $4 million.

And if her intent was to keep her cat-loving husband interested, it didn't work: Jocelyn filed for divorce in 1997 after catching Alec in bed with a Russian model, presumably fresh off the catwalk.

THE OLD BALLS GAME

I t's a baseball tradition to hand out free hats, shirts, and souvenir balls to fans. The Los Angeles Dodgers did this on August 10, 1995, gifting most of the 53,000 fans in attendance with a Dodgers-branded ball before a game against the St. Louis Cardinals. It was a routine day at the ballpark until the bottom of the ninth inning. The Cardinals led 2–1, and Cardinals pitcher Tom Henke struck out the Dodgers' Raul Mondesi, who was caught looking; Mondesi immediately argued the call with home plate umpire Jim Quick.

Dodgers manager Tommy Lasorda also came onto the field to argue with the umpire. Quick ejected both from the game. The crowd erupted, and reacted with the one tool at their disposal— thousands threw their baseballs onto the field. The Cardinals fled for the safety of the dugout until the barrage ended. After a few minutes they returned to the field... and then balls came flying out of the center-field bleachers. That was it—the umpires declared the game over, and, as is the rule in baseball, the home team, the Dodgers, forfeited.

"THOUSANDS THREW THEIR BASEBALLS ONTO THE FIELD."

COSTUME DRAMAS

CE-CREAM-KKKONE

It was a sunny day in Ocala, Florida, in 2012. Cars made their way along the main drag. Pedestrians walked to and from work and local eateries. And a bizarre Ku Klux Klan monster thingy stood in front of an ice-cream shop enthusiastically waving at passersby. Many of those passersby were outraged. One woman even called the ice-cream shop in tears to complain that she had to cross the street to avoid the jovial white supremacist. The owner of the shop, Liza Diaz, was confused by the uproar. She had never even heard of the "Ku Ku Klan" (as she described it to a reporter). All she knew is that her customers were gone and she was the scorn of the neighborhood. So what was all the hubbub about? Trying to drum up business, Diaz had hired a man to stand outside her shop wearing an ice-cream costume. "It's just an ice-cream cone!" she said. But the top of the vanilla cone looked a lot like a pointy KKK hood. Diaz threw the costume away.

MAYOR McMEAT

In a similar costume mishap, London's *Daily Mail* reported (as only they could), "Barmy councillor gives shocked onlookers the willies in costume that looks more like a terrifying eight-foot phallus than tasty banger." Translated into American, that goes: Jill Makinson-Sanders, mayor of Louth, Lincolnshire, England, dressed up in a sausage costume that made her look like a big pink penis. The 61-year-old mayor wanted to do something special when the Olympic torch was to be carried through her town in July 2012. So instead of wearing the traditional mayoral chain and robes, Makinson-Sanders decided to celebrate Louth's most popular export—sausage—by dressing up as one. To most of the embarrassed townsfolk, she looked like a giant pink Johnson running alongside the confused man carrying the Olympic torch.

SEXY BACKLASH

Ricky's, a costume superstore based in New York City, specializes in "sexy (fill-in-the-blank)" costumes. Many of these costumes generate complaints, none more so than a little black dress with a skeleton pattern that came with a measuring-tape ribbon belt and a measuring-tape choker chain. The name of the costume: Anna Rexia. The backlash was severe. "I'm just appalled," said Trish Jones-Bendel of the National Association of

Anorexia Nervosa & Associated Disorders, "because eating disorders have the highest mortality rate of any mental illness." Or, as one commenter said, "What's next—a 'Sexy Tumor' outfit?!" In 2011—two years after Anna Rexia became available—Ricky's pulled the costume.

NOBODY PUTS BABY IN A CORONER

The Sexy Jane Doe DOA costume brings new meaning to the phrase "death becomes her." Here's the actual description (typos preserved for your reading pleasure): "Although she doesn't have much of a personality, she is still drop dead gorgeous in this body bag dress, Im sure you have the personality and in this you will be gorgeous. Stretch satin mini dress with hood and a two way zipper front which can zip all the way up the hood. One breast has an outline of a body printed on to it an PROPERTY OF THE CORONER. Pack includes Coroners name tag fitted to a choker Jane Doe and matching fingerless gloves."

KING OF PAIN

King Richard the Lionheart of England was leading troops in battle in 1199 when he stopped a charge, hypnotized by an arrow fired at him by a French soldier. The arrow hit him in the shoulder, and he died of blood poisoning.

GRANT'S TOMB

The American economy was vibrant and healthy in 1969. Retail was an especially strong sector, and a new type of store was emerging: the discount variety chain, basically department store–size versions of five-and-dimes and neighborhood drugstores. Target, Walmart, and Kmart all began this way. One contemporary chain *not* around today is Grants, also known as W. T. Grant, founded as a dime store in Massachusetts in 1906. By the late 1960s, there were nearly 1,100 locations around the United States.

The overall financial health of the company, as well as that of the economy at large, led the Grants board of directors to expand the chain into new geographic areas, build bigger stores, and institute incentives to get people to shop at Grants, instead of at its biggest competitor, Kmart. The big idea was to offer store credit to its customers. Any customer. Any customer at all. While that immediately sounds bad, at the time, default rates on small loans, under $1,000, the kind of debt incurred at a store over time, were low. Grants thought they would make money on the deal.

Each store was given jurisdiction over its own credit system, and they lacked the record-keeping or resources to determine whether applicants were good credit risks or not. For example, no credit checks were done. Thousands of customers took advantage of this system to open credit lines at multiple Grants stores. Beyond that, Grants offered super-low repayment terms (interest rates under 5 percent) and plans with small minimum payments.

The American economy slowed down in 1970 and 1971, meaning people were paying their debt back even less, and certainly not to Grants. Few changes were made to the credit system, and by 1975 the company was bankrupt and closed its doors. Total amount of outstanding customer debt at that point: $276.3 million.

BATS OFF!

It's one of the most famous myths in rock music history...except that it's true. At a 1982 Ozzy Osbourne concert in Iowa, a fan threw what Osbourne assumed to be a rubber bat onstage. In a very heavy-metal gesture, Osbourne bit the head off of the rubber bat—except that it was a real bat. Blood spewed forth from the bat, and all over Osbourne and into his mouth. The singer had to undergo a round of rabies vaccinations.

AN ELEVATING TALE

Construction workers Edward Tyler, 26, and Wendell Amaker, 48, were doing renovation work at New York City's Staten Island Hotel one day in August 2011. They took an elevator between some of the old hotel's upper floors with a cart full of supplies—but the elevator door wouldn't open. They tried another floor—same thing. So they decided to ride the elevator to the basement to see if the doors would open there.

Shortly after passing the ground floor, the elevator car hit water. Tyler and Amaker were unaware that the city had been flooded by a storm that day—and that the hotel's basement was now basically a pool. The elevator stopped working and sank to the bottom of the shaft. Water started leaking into the car. Worse: The two men were the only people working in the hotel that day. Luckily, they were able to reach 911 by cell phone. Unluckily, they didn't know the hotel's address. All they could tell the operator was the name of the streets at a nearby intersection. Then the phone connection cut off.

New York City firefighters were soon in a mad scramble to find the trapped men. They got to the intersection and—on nothing more than a hunch—went to the Staten Island Hotel. But the security guard told them nobody was in the building. The firefighters persisted. They went to the rear of the building and saw a door that was ajar. They approached it...and heard screams. When they got to the car, Tyler and Amaker were standing on their supply cart, their heads three feet from the elevator's roof—and water up to their necks. It had been more than an hour since they had called 911. The firefighters dropped a narrow ladder into the car through an emergency hatch on the car's roof, and the trapped men were able to climb out of the car, their ordeal finally over.

Tyler and Amaker were taken to the firehouse, uninjured but badly shaken up. "They were happy to see us," FDNY captain James Melvin told reporters. "I think they thought the end was near." Asked why he and his men had chosen the hotel to check out first, Melvin answered with a shrug, "Lucky guess."

No surprises: A Norwegian man (unnamed in reports) found out that his surprise 40th birthday party was happening in a cabin in the woods in southern Norway. As the first of about 30 guests began to arrive, the birthday boy hid behind some trees near the house. He planned to surprise the friends who were there to surprise him: He took his shotgun and fired a round into the air. The first shot definitely surprised the partygoers. So did the second shot, which happened when the man emerged from his hiding spot, tripped, and accidentally fired. He shot one friend in the leg.

FUNNY MONEY

Nice tip. Dakoda Garren went to Rocky's Pizza in Battle Ground, Washington, in August 2012, and paid for his meal with coins, including a quarter—a 1930s Liberty Head quarter worth about $18,500. According to police, Garren had stolen the coin, along with several others, months earlier, and was spending them around town at face value, having no idea of their real worth. Garren was arrested on a charge of first-degree theft.

Unamused. Larry Jones bought an order of French fries at Darien Lake Theme Park in New York in September 2012, paying for it with a $50 bill. The cashier didn't like the look of the bill and called security. When they questioned Jones about the money, he showed them roughly $1,200 worth of $50 bills that he said he got as payment for a remodeling job he'd done. Then he stuffed a bunch of them into his mouth and tried to swallow them. Security officers were able to stop him. Jones was charged with possession of a forged instrument and tampering with physical evidence.

Cooking the books. In July 2012, a man in Sydney, Australia, sold his Toyota Supra for $15,000 in cash. He hid the cash in his oven "because his wife never used it." Sometime later his wife came home...and turned on the oven. (She was going to cook some chicken nuggets for their two children.) Australian bills are made from a plastic polymer, so the stacks of bills melted into lumps. Worse: The man had meant to use the cash the next day to make a mortgage payment—the couple was already behind on their payments—but the bills were so damaged that the bank wouldn't accept them. "It was everything I had," said the man, who was too embarrassed to have his identity made public.

Socked away. Dana Leland bought a pair of socks at a Rhode Island Target in November 2012 and paid for them with a $100 bill. The bill was counterfeit—and it was not exactly professionally made: It had Abraham Lincoln's face on it. (Real $100 bills carry Ben Franklin's face.) Police said Leland had gone into the same store three days in a row, buying items that cost less than $25 and paying for them with the Abraham Lincoln $100 bills. He was arrested.

Blank check. Leah Jarolimek was arrested at a gas station in Sheboygan, Wisconsin, in 2006, for trying to buy potato chips and cigarettes with what the clerk suspected was a counterfeit $20 bill. The tip-off? While the front looked like a normal bill, the back was totally blank. Jarolimek protested, claiming she had no idea the bill was bogus.

NO STRINGS ATTACHED

Philippe Quint is a Grammy-nominated classical concert violinist who routinely plays at such vaunted venues as Carnegie Hall and Lincoln Center. In 2008 he played a concert in Dallas, and after flying home he took a cab from the Newark Airport to his house. Unfortunately, he left something behind in the taxi: his violin. His $4 million, circa-1723 Stradivarius violin. Usually, when things get left in the back of a cab, they're gone forever, but amazingly, Quint's extremely valuable violin was tracked down by Newark police in just a few hours. Quint gave his cabbie, Mohammed Khalil, a $100 tip, and played an impromptu concert for about 50 drivers in the Newark Airport's taxi holding area.

The Stradivarius is synonymous with "priceless violin," but there are other great violin makes out there, such as Goffriller, made in Venice in the late 17th century. Robert Napier of Wiltshire, England, owned one with his four siblings, who inherited it from their mother, who played it during World War II as a member of a troop entertainment troupe called the Ebsworth Quartet. In 2008 Napier took the violin to a dealer in London, who appraised the instrument at £180,000 (about $280,000). Napier took the train back home, and after getting off at Taunton Station, he realized he no longer had the violin with him—he'd left it in the luggage rack by his seat. Despite a £10,000 reward and lots of press coverage, the violin never materialized.

Yo-Yo Ma is probably the most famous cellist in the world (go ahead, name another one). But even he isn't above losing a stringed instrument, even one as huge as a cello. In 1999 Ma took a cab to New York's Peninsula Hotel to prepare for a concert in Brooklyn. He put his cello in the cab's trunk, and when he arrived...he left it in the cab. The instrument was made in Venice in the 1730s and valued at about $2.5 million. Amazingly, police and Taxi and Limousine Commission workers found the instrument in a little over three hours—just in time for Ma to play his concert.

David Garrett is a classical violinist with pop music leanings—he has celebrity good looks (fans call him "the David Beckham of the violin") and he likes to do covers of Nirvana, Coldplay, and Michael Jackson songs in his stage shows, which are frequently broadcast on PBS. As one of the wealthiest and most notable violinists in the world, Garrett can afford to use only the best instruments, such as a Guadagnini. He had one until 2008. At the end of a concert at the Barbican Centre in London, he finished playing, went to walk off the stage, and tripped...falling onto his 236-year old, $1.2 million instrument.

HOW MUCH WOOD *COULD* A WOODCHUCK CHUCK?

The Abenaki Indians of what is now New England considered the woodchuck their maternal ancestor, "a wise grandmother who taught them to fish, hunt, and build canoes," according to nature writer Sy Montgomery. The beloved—and relatively rare—rodents generally kept to the woods. But when white settlers arrived, they cleared the woods, killed the woodchuck's predators, and planted crops that happened to be the kinds of foods that wood-chucks, also known as groundhogs, loved to eat.

Suddenly, woodchuck populations exploded and the little guys that once seemed so wise and cute now seemed a bit less of both. This is not entirely surprising; animals that eat and dig as much as a woodchuck don't often make friends among farmers. Soon enough, pretty much every-one in New England agreed that woodchucks were awful and far, far too plentiful. In 1883 the New Hampshire Legislative Woodchuck Committee de-clared the woodchuck "absolutely destitute of any interesting qualities." As a result of the commit-tee's thorough investigation, the legislature moved to offer a bounty for each dead woodchuck the citizens of the state could procure.

BAD, SANTA

Up on the housetop. When Santa grew that beard of his all those centuries ago, he didn't think about how it would affect his rappelling. But he learned the hard way one warm November night in 2007. At a Christmas tree–lighting ceremony in front of a Conroe, Texas, shopping mall, Santa was all set to emerge from the top of the 80-foot-high sign and rappel down the brick wall. The dozens of revelers chanted, "Santa! Santa! Santa!" And then Santa (aka rock climber James Bosson) emerged and started his descent. But his beard got stuck in a latch. Try as he might, Santa couldn't free himself. The kids were getting anxious. Finally, someone tossed a knife up to Santa and he started cutting. As white, fluffy bits and pieces of beard fell to the ground, it almost seemed as if it was snowing in Texas. But try as he might, the beardless Santa couldn't get the hair out of the latch; he wasn't going anywhere. Eventually, the fire department came and freed him. And Santa learned a valuable lesson about beards and rappelling.

Here comes Santa Claus. It happened again in 2011 at a shopping mall in Palm Beach Gardens, Florida. Throngs of children were awaiting Santa's grand entrance from the three-story-high ceiling. "Here he is!" said the mall announcer over the intercom. The kids cheered when a harnessed St. Nick began rappelling down. Then his beard got tangled in the ropes. As he was struggling and wiggling, the announcer tried to get everyone to join her in a rendition of "We Wish You a Merry Christmas," but the kids were transfixed on the dangling Santa. "Magic can happen," she said. "Magic can happen if you guys sing!" Magic didn't happen. Quite the opposite, actually, when Santa had to remove his hat—revealing a head of brown hair. Some of the children screamed. Santa finally got down, but by that point, the magic was all gone.

Christmas wrapping. Santa did it again a year later at the Broad Street Mall in Reading, England. This time, Father Christmas (as they call him in the UK) was played by British soldier Steve Chessell. On his way down to the floor, his beard got impossibly stuck. After it became clear that Chessell wasn't going anywhere, the jovial mall announcer asked, "Father Christmas, are you going to stay up there, Father Christmas?" Father Christmas gave a sheepish wave. "Well," said the announcer to laughter, "shall we go on and switch on the lights anyway?" So they did, and everyone enjoyed themselves while Santa and his tangled beard hung over them like a Christmas ornament. Forty minutes later, another soldier (in camo, so he was hard to see) rappelled down and freed Santa.

Santa baby. Christmas Day 2007 ended badly for one Santa. He got drunk and decided to take a joyride through Hollywood. When police arrested him in front of Grauman's Chinese Theatre, he was wearing a Santa hat, plus "a wig, a red lace camisole, and a purple G-string." Quipped one deputy: "We're pretty sure this isn't the real Santa."

It must be Santa. In 1999, during an otherwise ho-ho-ho-hum afternoon of kids demanding stuff from St. Nick, a mom named Kelley Fornatoro placed her baby on the big man's lap at a Woodland Hills, California, shopping mall. The baby started crying. "Why don't you put your arm around him to calm him down?" Fornatoro suggested. Santa (whose name wasn't released) grudgingly sat for the photo. When Fornatoro went to retrieve her baby, Santa asked, "Was it worth it? Was it worth it for you to torture your child for a picture? You must be an evil person!" Fornatoro called him rude. "You shouldn't be around children," she added. She then threatened to file a complaint with the mall manager. "You can complain about me if you want, but I am Santa Claus!" replied the man who was not Santa Claus. "I am the best person in the world! I am good!" He then started pulling off his Santa garb—hat, wig, beard, coat, belt—piece by piece, flinging them this way and that. Then—as parents covered their traumatized children's eyes—mall cops arrived and escorted the tank-top-clad former Santa away.

NEARLY NUCLEAR WARS

Late on the night of October 25, 1962, a guard at an Air Force base in Minnesota spotted a dark figure climbing the fence surrounding the base. The guard shot and killed the mysterious figure. The fence was wired to detect intruders, and the culprit's fall set off the alarm. But the fence was incorrectly wired, and the alarm set off a second alarm hundreds of miles away at an Air National Guard base in Wisconsin. F-106 fighter jets armed with nuclear missiles immediately prepared to take off toward the Soviet Union in response to the intrusion. But the nuclear strike was quickly called off after an investigation determined the identity of the fence-climbing spy: It was a bear.

On January 25, 1995, a team of Norwegian and American scientists launched a research rocket off the northwest coast of Norway. It contained equipment to collect data on the aurora borealis, or northern lights. The rocket was noticed by radar operators at the Olengorsk early-warning station in Russia, who mistakenly identified the small, unarmed rocket as a submarine-launched nuclear Trident missile headed for Moscow. The news was sent to Russian president Boris Yeltsin, who, for a moment, was ready to hit the "launch nukes" button. Fortunately, minutes later, the radar operators noticed that the "missile" was heading away from Russia, and determined that it wasn't really a threat. The rocket collected its data and landed safely on an Arctic island a half hour later. Ironically, the scientists had notified the Russian government of the rocket launch weeks in advance, but the information had not made its way to the early-warning radar operators or Yeltsin.

On November 9, 1979, computers at three American military control centers all displayed the same grim news: Soviet nuclear missiles were on their way. Officers immediately put missile launch sites on alert, and 10 fighter jets took off to shoot down anything suspicious. However, before launching a counterstrike, officers at the three bases decided to back up the information they'd received. Satellite data across the country showed no signs of Soviet missiles in the air. It turns out that a training tape of attack scenarios had been placed into the computer running the military's early-warning system.

BOTCHED BUNGEE

On a clear Sunday morning in Perris, California, in 1991, bungee jumping instructor Hal Irish went up in a hot-air balloon to do a demonstration jump for his students. He secured one end of the cord to the basket, the other end to his harness. Then he took the plunge. The cord extended to its full length before gently pulling Irish back up in the air, but somehow the harness became disconnected from the cord... and Irish kept sailing up into the air before he fell back down 70 feet to his death—the first fatality in bungee jumping.

• Erin Langworthy, an Australian college student, and her friend were backpacking through Africa on New Year's Eve 2011 when they decided to go whitewater rafting and then bungee jumping at Victoria Falls in Zambia. Langworthy was secured to the cord on a bridge 365 feet above the Zambezi River. She jumped off and spread her arms like she was supposed to, and then the cord snapped and Langworthy hit the water hard. She was able to shield her head with her arms just before impact. Next thing she knew, she was caught in the rapids with 20 feet of the cord still attached to her ankles...which were also attached to each other. Remembering a lesson from that morning's rafting trip, Langworthy put her feet in front of her to avoid hitting the rocks. She tried to get to the riverbank, but the cord became snagged on something—she actually had to swim under the water to free it, twice. She then made her way to the riverbank, where rescuers treated for severe bruises, a broken collarbone, and damaged lungs. "I felt like I'd been slapped all over," said Langworthy. She said she's not in any hurry to try a second bungee jump. The icing on the cake: Langworthy landed in "crocodile-infested waters" (even though no crocs had been spotted that day).

• In May 2002, Alberto Galletti and his girlfriend, Tiziana Accorra, arrived at Lorenzo Illuminati's Umbria, Italy, bungee-jumping park, but it was late and Illuminati had closed for the day. The couple begged him to reopen; Galletti, a member of Italy's elite Folgore army parachute regiment, really wanted to take Accorra, a college student, on her first bungee jump. Illuminati agreed, but only if the couple paid an extra fee. They paid up and got strapped in for a tandem bungee jump off a bridge that had seen thousands of jumps without incident...until this one. Tragically, not one but both snap hooks opened when the cord reached full length, and the lovebirds died together.

HELLO, DOLLY

I n May 2011, on his very last day of high school, 18-year-old Tyell Morton of Rushville, Indiana, put on a hooded sweatshirt to hide his face from security cameras, entered his high school carrying a large cardboard box, and went into a girls' restroom. He opened the package—took a life-size sex doll out of it, propped the doll up inside a stall, and left.

Security staff saw a hooded figure enter the school with a large box and leave again a short time later without the box—and immediately called the bomb squad and evacuated the building. It was several hours before the sex doll was discovered. An investigation led to Morton, and he admitted what he'd done, explaining that it was a senior prank. The response: Prosecutor Phil Caviness charged him with institutional criminal mischief—a felony that carries a sentence of up to eight years in prison.

After public outcry from all over the country—there were even "Free Tyell" websites set up—Caviness eventually agreed to a diversion program that would see Tyell's charges dropped if he stayed out of trouble for one year. Tyell, who had never been in trouble with the law, met the requirement in August 2012—and his prank was finally over.

DEAD MUSICIANS

Jeff Buckley (1966–97). The up-and-coming rock star was in Memphis, Tennessee, to record some new music with his band. On the night before recording was to begin, Buckley decided to take a swim in one of his favorite spots in the North River Harbor along the Mississippi River. A roadie, Keith Foti, was there with him, but opted to stay dry. Buckley was in a good mood, though, and jumped in the water fully clothed—heavy boots and all. He was doing the backstroke while singing Led Zeppelin's "Whole Lotta Love" when the wake from a passing tugboat approached. Foti turned away to shield a guitar from the wave. When he turned back around, Buckley was gone. His body was found five days later.

Chet Baker (1929–88). Baker was an influential jazz trumpeter and singer whose life was marred by heroin addiction and prison time. After his career had stalled, he was making a comeback in 1988, and he was having a pretty good year—musically, anyway. Baker was still struggling with drug addiction. He was staying in an Amsterdam hotel room by himself...and a lot of heroin and cocaine. In the middle of the night, Baker opened the window of the second-story room. Somehow, he fell out and hit his head on a metal post and died. The death was ruled an accident, not a suicide—there was no note. And who tries to kill himself by jumping out of a second-story window?

Les Harvey (1945–72). Ever heard of the Scottish band Stone the Crows? They might have been a lot more popular had a stagehand at the Top Rank Ballroom in Swansea, Wales, been more careful. While setting up for 1972 show, he plugged a microphone cable into an improperly wired amplifier. During the sound check, lead guitarist Les Harvey, whose hands were wet, grabbed the microphone. It was not grounded; Harvey was. He was electrocuted and died instantly.

Terry Kath (1946–78). In 1978 Kath, the original front man for the band Chicago, and his wife were partying at a roadie's house in Woodland Hills, California. Kath loved guns, and he had two of his favorite pistols with him. At one point, he placed the barrel of a .38 revolver on his temple and pulled the trigger several times. Click, click, click. Nothing happened. Then Kath picked up his semiautomatic 9 mm pistol. "Don't worry," he assured them. "It's not loaded." He even showed them the empty magazine to prove it. But Kath didn't check the chamber. There was bullet in it. He put the pistol up to his temple, pulled the trigger, and died.

Randy Rhoads (1956–82). A guitarist for Quiet Riot, Rhoads was also Ozzy Osbourne's lead guitarist. During a tour stopover at the Leesburg, Florida, estate where Ozzy's bus driver, Andrew Aycock, lived, Rhoads reluctantly agreed to take a short flight in a 1955 Beechcraft Bonanza. Rhoads was afraid of flying, but he was persuaded to go up because the other passenger, hairdresser Rachel Youngblood, had a heart condition, so Aycock promised not to do anything too scary. But Aycock did do something scary: He buzzed the tour bus where several band members were sleeping. After two successful buzzes, Aycock looped back around for a third one. But he got way too close, and the Beechcraft's wing clipped the back of the bus. The plane spun out of control, took out the top of a tree, and then crashed into the mansion's garage. It exploded into a ball of fire, and all three passengers were burned alive.

Johnny Ace (1929–54). Ace, a well-known blues singer in the 1950s, was touring with Big Mama Thornton's band. Between sets of a Christmas Day gig in Houston, Texas, Ace, Thornton, and the rest of the band were sitting around a table. As he often did, Ace pulled out his .22 caliber revolver. He was drinking, which he also often did. According to bass player Curtis Tillman, "He had this little pistol he was waving around the table and someone said, 'Be careful with that thing.' And Johnny Ace said, 'It's okay! Gun's not loaded, see?' And he pointed it at himself with a smile on his face, and 'Bang!' Sad, sad thing.' "

Once upon a time, there was a rock star who really liked having clean underwear when he was on tour. One night, in order to get to a gig early so he'd have enough time to wash his clothes, he skipped the tour bus and chartered a plane. He also footed the tickets for two of his tour mates, one who had the flu and another who won the last seat in a coin toss. It was February 1959. Ritchie Valens won the coin toss (over Waylon Jennings), the Big Bopper had the flu, and Buddy Holly needed fresh skivvies. The plane crashed; all on board were killed.

UP IN THE AIR

As it approached Singapore's Changi Airport in 2010, operations were normal on Jetstar flight JQ57. Just before the plane began its descent, the pilot decided that he could turn his cell phone on and check his text messages. As the plane started to nosedive, the copilot warned his pilot that the plane was about to crash; no reply. With 392 feet left before sudden impact, the copilot realized that the pilot had neglected to lower the landing gear. It was too late to release it, so the copilot grabbed the yoke and pushed the plane back into the air, then circled and landed the plane safely. Jetstar officials plan to put warnings about cell phone use in all pilot training materials.

RUSSIAN HIT MAN GONE WRONG

In early 2012, videographers Jonathan Vanegas and Vitaly Zdorovetskiy made a video called "Miami Zombie Attack Prank." In it, Zdorovetskiy dressed in disheveled clothes smeared with red goop, walked around neighborhoods in Miami scaring people while Vanegas filmed. It was viewed more than 13 million times on YouTube. Their follow-up was another prank video called "Russian Hit Man Prank Gone Wrong." Vanegas, dressed in a suit and tie, walks through a supermarket parking lot carrying a briefcase and talking on a cell phone. He approaches a middle-aged man, puts the briefcase down in front of him, and tells him he has 60 seconds to run away. The man, terrified, runs alongside Zdorovetskiy. Zdorovetskiy keeps acting like he's talking to someone on the cell phone, stopping, then running again, the terrified man right there with him. After a minute or so he finally tells the man it's a prank and that he's simply filming him with his camera phone.

The man did not take it well. He kicked and punched Zdorovetskiy, then chased him to where Vanegas was still filming the two. "You trying to get a laugh?" he screamed at the two. "I'm not a motherf— you laugh at!" He then landed a couple punches on Vanegas, yelling, "If you keep filming me, I am going to f— you up!" The video goes on for a few more minutes, with the guy screaming profanities at the two pranksters, and the pranksters apologizing. It finally ends with Zdorovetskiy muttering, "We gotta go."

> **"MEANWHILE, SOMEONE HAD CALLED THE COPS— AND THEY SOON ARRIVED WITH A BOMB SQUAD."**

Meanwhile, someone had called the cops—and they soon arrived with a bomb squad. Zdorovetskiy fled, but Vanegas was arrested on felony bomb hoax charges and spent the night in jail. Zdorovetskiy was later arrested on the same charges. The victim of the prank was identified as 51-year-old Air Force veteran Andre Brown. He told reporters that he thought Zdorovetskiy and Vanegas should not be severely punished, saying, "I think they need to think about what they're doing more carefully." Brown was not charged with any crimes.

BETTER SAFE THAN SORRY

In 1947 Olga Frankevich and her sister fled from Soviet police during a purge of anti-Communist dissidents. The Frankeviches took up residence in a house in rural Ukraine. They were too afraid to come out...until 1992. Olga hid under the bed almost the entire time. Her sister moved about the house.

UNACCEPTABLE

Vassar College sends out acceptance e-mails to applicants around the world in lieu of the traditional postal letter. But in January 2012, 122 early-application hopefuls were informed by e-mail of their upcoming matriculation at the prestigious institution. Unfortunately, only 46 of those students had actually been accepted. Vassar's computer system had set up a placeholder "test" acceptance e-mail, which, because of a computer error, was accidentally sent to everyone on the applicant list, regardless of their status.

• **Cornell University** is an Ivy League school, so it's hard to get into and hard to pay for. In 2009 somebody in the financial-aid office used the wrong mailing list and sent 25 already rejected applicants a letter telling them that they had been accepted and needed to fill out financial-aid paperwork.

• **In 2007 the University of North Carolina at Chapel Hill** sent a letter out to all 2,700-odd freshman applicants informing them of their acceptance. The college hadn't even decided who it was going to accept yet.

• **In 2009 the University of California San Diego,** sent welcome letters to 28,000 applicants who had previously been told of their rejection and even included an invitation to a summer orientation weekend. A few hundred students and their families showed up, thinking the college had somehow reversed their rejections.

"A FEW HUNDRED STUDENTS AND THEIR FAMILIES SHOWED UP, THINKING THE COLLEGE HAD SOMEHOW REVERSED THEIR REJECTIONS."

• **The University of California, Los Angeles,** accepts thousands of freshmen, but also maintains a waiting list in case spots open up. In April 2012, the school's admissions office emailed financial-aid updates to thousands of newly admitted students...as well as the 894 students on the waiting list. The letter concluded with the line, "Once again congratulations on your admission to UCLA," which wasn't true, along with a link to their financial-aid profile, clearly marked "waiting list." Confused students were issued an apology two days later.

• **The Diversity Visa Program (also called the Green Card Lottery)** issues 50,000 visas annually to people from nations with low U.S. immigration rates, particularly in Africa and the Middle East. Around 13 million people apply for the program annually, requiring a lottery, conducted at random by computer. In 2011, 22,000 applicants were selected too early in the process, and received "Welcome to America!" letters...before the State Department had to apologize and backtrack.

DOWN ON THE FARM

In November 1995, farmer Lowell Altvater, 80, of Sandusky, Ohio, saw a rat in his barn and fired his shotgun at it. Except it wasn't a rat—it was his wife's hat. And she was wearing it at the time. She was behind a divider wall in the barn, and Mr. Altvater, seeing only the hat above it, mistook it for a rat scurrying along the top of the wall. Mrs. Altvater was not hurt, but her husband was charged with negligent assault anyway, partly, police said, because just a few years earlier Mr. Altvater had shot himself in the leg in the same barn...while trying to shoot a rat.

• In October 2011, John Watkyn-James, 51, was driving his tractor down a rural road in the south of Wales, towing a metal work trailer roughly 10 feet long, when he parked on the road near one of his pastures to feed some horses. Big no-no: He parked with the trailer straddling a train track. Less than a minute later a high-speed passenger train hit the trailer at roughly 75 mph. The trailer was smashed to bits, and the nose of the train was heavily damaged, but, very fortunately, the train did not derail, and nobody was hurt. Watkyn-James was, however, charged with "endangering the safety of persons using the railway," and was ordered to perform 200 hours of community service. He was also told by the judge that he was "incredibly stupid."

• In November 2012, a farmer on the outskirts of Billings, Montana, was driving a combine harvester through his cornfield when he felt a "shudder" go through the machine. He shut the harvester off and, in what could have been a scene from a horror film, found a screaming man caught up  in the machine's giant cylinder of blades. When emergency medical technicians finally arrived, they had to manually reverse the blades to get the man out. Amazingly, he was pretty much okay: He needed lots of stitches, but none of his injuries were life-threatening. How did the guy end up in the harvester? The 57-year-old, who police said they would not be identifying, told officers that he'd been walking down a nearby road when he'd gotten tired...and decided to lie down in the cornfield. He fell asleep—and the combine had driven right over him, snagging him by his clothes and pulling him up into the blades. "The man is incredibly lucky to be alive," Sheriff Kent O'Donnell said. "And that's about all you can say about that."

"WE REGRET THE ERROR"

There was an error in the Dear Abby column that was published on Monday. In the fifth paragraph, the second sentence stated that Charlie's hiccups were cured temporarily through the use of carbon monoxide. It should have read carbon dioxide."

—Anchorage Daily News

"In our entry on Garrison Keillor's *Lake Wobegon Days*, we referred to *A Prairie Ho Companion*; we meant *A Prairie Home Companion*."

—The Guardian (U.K.)

"In an article in Monday's newspaper, there may have been a misperception about why a Woodstock man is going to Afghanistan on a voluntary mission. Kevin DeClark is going to Afghanistan to gain life experience to become a police officer when he returns, not to 'shoot guns and blow things up.' "

—The Sentinel-Review
(Woodstock, Ontario, Canada)

"An earlier version of this story incorrectly described Buffington's special support hose as 'mercury-lined.' The hose are mercury-gauged, meaning that barometric mercury is used to measure the compression of the hose. They are not mercury-lined, which would, of course, make them poisonous."

—*The Sunday Paper* (Atlanta, Georgia)

"In our feature 'Why She Left Him,' the woman identified in the photograph as former adult-film star Ginger Lynn Allen is neither Ms. Allen nor an adult-film actress. *US* regrets the error."

—*US Weekly*

"A story on Wednesday about foraging for edible mushrooms contained a photo of *Amanita muscaria*, which is a poisonous and hallucinogenic mushroom. It was a copyeditor's error."

—*Portland* (Maine) *Press Herald*

"We misspelled the word 'misspelled' twice, as 'mispelled,' in the Corrections and Clarifications column on September 26, page 30."

—*The Guardian*

THE EDGE OF OLYMPIC GLORY

Athlete: Thomas Hamilton-Brown

Event: Boxing, lightweight division

Story: At the 1936 Summer Olympics in Berlin, South African boxer Hamilton-Brown lost his first-round fight to Chile's Carlos Lillo in a split decision, and he was out of the Games. But a couple of days later, Olympic officials announced that the judges had made a scoring error—and that Hamilton-Brown was the winner of the fight. However, after his loss, Hamilton-Brown had consoled himself with an eating binge. When it came time to fight his next match—the one he didn't think was coming—he was five pounds over his weight-class limit. Hamilton-Brown was disqualified.

Athlete: Siegfried "Wim" Esajas

Event: 800-meter run

Story: At the 1960 Summer Olympics in Rome, Esajas became the first athlete from Suriname to compete in the Olympics. Or he would have been. Esajas overslept on the day of his qualifying heat and missed the race. It turns out the blunder wasn't his fault. Suriname's Olympic Committee later admitted that its secretary-general, Fred Glans, had incorrectly told Esajas that his race had been rescheduled from the morning to the afternoon.

Athletes: Eddie Hart and Rey Robinson

Event: 100-meter dash

Story: At the 1972 Summer Olympics, Americans Hart and Robinson were the favorites to win gold and silver in the 100-meter dash. On the morning of August 31, they both made it handily through their heats, and qualified for the quarterfinals, to be held that evening. While Hart, Robinson, and their coach, Stan Wright, were on a stroll that afternoon, they saw races being shown on a television screen in the Olympic Village. At first they thought it was a replay of their morning races, but then they saw a race about to start with Hart's name listed for it...with an "N/A" next to it. The quarterfinals were being held *now.* The three ran (really fast, we imagine) to the stadium, but they were too late. Hart and Robinson missed their races and were immediately disqualified. Wright was blamed for the fiasco at first, but the U.S. Olympic Committee later admitted that Wright had been given a race schedule that was later changed, and he had not been notified. Hart and Robinson went home empty-handed and never made it to the Olympics again.

Athletes: Olympic torchbearers

Event: Lighting the Olympic flame

Story: During the opening ceremonies at the 1988 Summer Olympics in Seoul, South Korea, hundreds of live "Doves of Peace" were released into the packed Olympic stadium, an Olympic tradition going back to 1920. The doves are supposed to be released just as the Olympic flame is being lit, but, for reasons unknown, this time they were released several minutes beforehand. Where did the doves go? Dozens landed on the soon-to-be-lit Olympic cauldron. Minutes later, as the huge crowd looked on, the three Olympic torchbearers—who could plainly see all the birds on the cauldron—lit the flame. And a bunch of Doves of Peace became barbecued Doves of Peace. Furious protests by animal-rights groups followed, apologies were issued, and releasing live doves during opening ceremonies lasted just one more Olympics before the practice ended.

Athlete: Lindsey Jacobellis

Event: Snowboard cross

Story: At the 2006 Winter Olympics, American snowboarder Jacobellis was almost 50 yards ahead of her nearest competitor with about 100 yards to go in the women's snowboard cross final. On the second-to-last jump, Jacobellis made an early-celebration showboating move—and fell straight on her rear end when she landed. She scrambled to her feet and tried to make it to the finish line in first place, but the snowboarder who had been so far behind her, Switzerland's Tanja Frieden, swooped by—and won the race by a comfortable three-second margin. In postrace interviews, Jacobellis said she hadn't been show-boating—she'd only been trying to stabilize herself in the air. She later admitted that she *had* been showboating.

Athletes: North Korean women's soccer team

Event: Before a match

Story: In the minutes before the 2012 Summer

Olympics match between the North Korean and Colombian women's soccer teams, the North Korean players looked up to see their faces and names on the jumbo screens around the stadium. Alongside the team photos was an image of a flag—the flag of South Korea. Outraged North Korean players stormed off the field and refused to play. Panicked officials could be seen on the sidelines trying to calm players and coaches as the video crew worked to get the right flag on the screens. Finally—after 40 minutes—they did, and the game began. London's Olympic Committee was forced to issue formal apologies—even British Prime Minister David Cameron apologized for the gaffe. An Olympic Committee spokesman later said the error had been made by a London video producer (whom they declined to name).

SWITCHING CHANNELS

THE CASH COW

Back in the late 1960s, pro football wasn't the overwhelmingly popular sport it is today. In those days, it enjoyed mostly regional popularity in the upper Midwest and Northeast. But the two leagues, the AFL and NFL, merged in 1966, consolidating resources just as the sport was becoming far more popular. NFL commissioner Pete Rozelle knew that a weekly TV game would increase exposure and take the sport national—and Major League Baseball already televised games nationally. Rozelle approached CBS and NBC, the #1 and #2 networks. Because of that, they weren't looking to give up three hours of prime-time programming each week for a sport that wouldn't draw as many viewers as shows like *Laugh-In* or *My Three Sons*.

There were only three networks then, so Rozelle went to third-place ABC...which had nothing to lose. They agreed to air a weekly NFL game on Monday nights, and in fall 1970, *Monday Night Football* debuted. Not only did it help popularize pro football in the United States, it made billions for ABC and was a Top-20 show for most of its run. It moved to ESPN in 2006.

THE CLASSIC

In the early '80s, the hottest thing going on broadcast TV were soaps like *Dynasty* and *Dallas*, and action shows like The *A-Team*

"WHAT SHOW WAS REJECTED BY ABC, CBS, NBC, UPN, AND MTV?"

and *Simon & Simon*. What wasn't popular? Situation comedies. In the 1982–83 season, there was only one comedy in the Nielsen Top 10: *Three's Company*, on ABC. The unpopularity of sitcoms was one of the reasons why ABC entertainment president Lewis Erlicht personally rejected a pitch from enduringly popular comedian Bill Cosby for a comedy about an upper-middle-class African American family. Another reason was that Cosby wanted a full commitment from the network—he wanted a guarantee the show would air without his having to submit a script or produce a pilot episode. In his assessment, Erlicht wrote that the show "lacked bite," and that "viewers wouldn't watch an unrealistic portrayal of blacks as wealthy, well educated professionals." He was quite wrong. *The Cosby Show* debuted on third-place NBC in fall 1984. That season it was the #3 show on TV... and for the next five seasons it was the #1 show on TV, launching NBC into first place.

THE JUGGERNAUT

What show was rejected by ABC, CBS, NBC, UPN, and MTV, only to be accepted by Fox as a low-key summer replacement? *American Idol*, the #1 show on TV for seven straight years, and which generates nearly $1 billion in revenue a year for Fox.

MILITARY MINDLESSNESS

I n the 1450s, the gunsmith Urban of Hungary crafted "the Basilica," the largest cannon ever built. The 19-ton behemoth required 100 men to move and could shoot an 800-pound cannonball over a mile. Urban tried to sell the Basilica to Byzantine emperor Constantine XI, but Constantine turned him down on grounds that the cannon was too expensive. So Urban sold it to Ottoman Turk leader Sultan Mehmed II, who used the cannon to blow down the walls of Constantinople in 1453 and take the city from Constantine XI.

• Hitler left the defense of France's Channel Coast to one of his top commanders, Erwin Rommel. On the night of June 5, 1944, things were so quiet and safe, Rommel decided to head home to Germany and surprise his wife for her birthday.
  The next day was D-Day.

• John Sedgwick, a major general for the Union during the Civil War, found the Confederate sniper attacks at the Battle of Spotsylvania to be wanting. "What! What! Men dodging this way from a single bullet! I am ashamed of you. They couldn't hit an elephant at this dist—" were reportedly Sedgwick's last words.

FIRE THE WRITER

In 1896 publisher Alfred Harmsworth founded the *London Daily Mail*, which is still in print today. He held reporters to a very high standard, but liked to check in with them to see if they enjoyed their work. He once asked his staff if they were happy working for him. One reporter, attempting to tell Harmsworth what he thought he wanted to hear, said, "Yes, sir." Harmsworth immediately fired him, telling the reporter, "I don't want anyone here to be content on five pounds a week."

In April 2012, Khristopher Brooks was offered what he called a "dream job": a position as a reporter for the *Wilmington News Journal* in Delaware. He was so happy he wrote a story about the hire—written as though it were a *News Journal* press release—and put it on his blog. A week later, the editor of the paper called Brooks. He'd seen the "press release," he said, and Brooks was guilty of "illegal use of the company logo" in it, as well as the improper quoting of a section of the letter offering him the job. Result: The job offer was rescinded.

(NOSE) CANDY

On Halloween 2012, Donald Green was at his girlfriend's house in Royton, England, handing out candy to trick-or-treaters. Three little kids came to the door, and Green reached into his pocket for bags of Gummi Bears that his girlfriend had given him to hand out. But Green reached into the wrong pocket and grabbed three little baggies of cocaine, and dropped *those* into the trick-or-treaters' goody bags.

The kids' father, it turned out, was an off-duty police officer, so when he saw his children playing with little baggies of coke later that evening, he confiscated the drugs. "Where did you get these?" he asked. "At the last house we went to," replied his daughter.

Meanwhile, back at the girlfriend's house, Green reached into his pocket for the drugs (which he'd purchased earlier that day for £200) and discovered his mistake. In a panic he drove all over town looking for the kids, but couldn't find them. So he went back to his girlfriend's house, and not long after, the police showed up. "I know why you're here," Green said sadly after he opened the door. He was arrested and sentenced to 130 hours of community service.

CAUGHT ON GOOGLE STREET VIEW

After photographing several UK cities for Street View, Google fielded hundreds of complaints from citizens who inadvertently wound up in photos—including a man caught exiting a sex shop, a man throwing up outside of a pub, and a group of teenagers getting arrested.

• Sharp-eyed Google Earth users noticed a collection of 40-year-old buildings in Southern California that, from above, resembled a Nazi swastika. The owner of the structures: the U.S. Navy (the buildings were barracks on a military base). The Navy spent $600,000 to redesign the facility.

• While photographing for Street View in Melbourne, Australia, Google's car-mounted cameras captured a man passed out in the street in front of his mother's house. The man, who'd had too much to drink after a funeral, later complained. Google removed the photos.

• Users scrolling through pictures of upstate New York on Street View noticed a fawn standing in the middle of a rural road. But in subsequent shots, the deer was lying in the road, dead, with blood-soaked tire tracks leading away from it. Google's camera car, it turned out, had accidentally hit it. The company kept the images but edited out the deer.

• If you look closely, you can spot hundreds of photos that caught people urinating in public, including one with a French bus driver photographed relieving himself on the side of his bus.

• One female Google Earth user was looking at photos of a girlfriend's house—and spotted her own husband's Range Rover out front. Divorce proceedings followed.

* * 📌 * *

ALMOST PRESIDENT

After a failed presidential run in 1836, Whig leader and former senator William Henry Harrison was selected by his party's convention to run for president again in 1840. This time, he won. The race for vice president, however, ended in a tie between Senator John Tyler and convention chairman John Janney. Janney, doing the gracious and honorable thing, stepped aside as convention leader and ceded the VP slot to Tyler. Then Harrison died after 32 days in office, having caught pneumonia at his own inauguration. Tyler became the new president, a role he technically won by a single vote: Janney's.

McWHAT?

I n its ongoing effort to get every human alive to eat at McDonald's, the fast-food giant's ad team erected a billboard in St. Paul, Minnesota, with a picture of an Egg McMuffin and a cup of hot coffee next to these words:

Yuavtxhawbpabraukojsawv yuavntxivzograukoj mus

A bewildering string of gibberish? Yes, especially in the language it's supposedly written in. The text was Hmong, to appeal to St. Paul's Hmong community, an ethnicity from the mountainous regions spanning China, Vietnam, Laos, and Thailand.

The ad backfired. That's because whoever translated the words into Hmong botched the spelling, grammar, syntax, and punctuation. It was supposed to say, "Coffee Gets You Up, Breakfast Gets You Going." But in Hmong, it read something like "Coffee up you, breakfast go you." Or, more accurately, "coffeeupyou breakfastgoyou," because the sign didn't include the spaces that go between words in most languages, including Hmong.

A McDonald's spokesperson apologized for the nonsensical billboard. Then they fixed it so that it made sense in Hmong.

MORE POLITICAL GAFFES

A stand-up guy. In September 2008, vice-presidential candidate Joe Biden was speaking at a rally in Columbia, Missouri, when he began going through a list of names of local politicians who were in attendance, thanking them from the stage and getting the crowd to cheer for them. "Chuck Graham, state senator, is here," Biden said, as the crowd cheered wildly. "Stand up, Chuck. Let 'em see ya!" Biden yelled into the microphone. Then he went, "Oh!" and his face visibly dropped. Oops: Graham is a paraplegic and makes use of a wheelchair. Biden did his best to recover, saying, "God love ya. What am I talking about?" Then he asked the *crowd* to "stand up for Chuck," which the crowd awkwardly did.

You're fired. In October 2000, German chancellor Gerhard Schröder was invited by Israeli premier Ehud Barak to visit the Yad Vashem Holocaust Museum in Jerusalem. When Barak and Schröder came to the museum's Eternal Flame memorial for the six million Jews killed in the Holocaust, Barak, in a somber and symbolic gesture, invited the German leader to turn a handle that would make the eternal flame grow in strength.

Schröder turned the handle...the wrong way. The flame went out. Barak tried to help Schröder correct the mistake, to no avail. (A technician relit the flame.)

He got beat. Newly elected Australian Liberal Party leader Alexander Downer, in line to be the country's next prime minister, gave a speech at a 1994 formal dinner in Sydney. Downer began to talk up his party's new "The Things That Matter" slogan. He started off with a joke, quipping that he was thinking of calling his anti–domestic violence initiative "The Things That Batter." The crowd, which included several prominent female Australian politicians—and many Australians, since the event was televised—reacted with silent shock. Within months Downer was no longer leader of the Liberal Party. His eight months in the position is still the shortest term in the party's history.

Darkest Portugal. On February 11, 2011, India's foreign minister, S. M. Krishna, gave his very first speech before the United Nations Security Council in New York. A full three minutes into his speech, India's envoy to the U.N. stepped forward, took the script from Krishna's hands, and gave him another one. "You can start again," he muttered before stepping away. The problem: Krishna had been reading the speech already given by the foreign minister of Portugal, left on top of Krishna's papers by the Portuguese foreign minister. Krishna's aides later tried to laugh off the gaffe, saying the beginning portion of the speech contained mostly pleasantries that any speech might have had, and that it could have happened to anyone. But probably not; among the lines Krishna read was, "Allow me to express my profound satisfaction regarding the happy coincidence of having two Portuguese-speaking countries here today." (At which point chuckling could be heard in the room.)

It's Finnished. In July 2005, French president Jacques Chirac attended a dinner in Kaliningrad, Russia, and at some point during the evening made what he thought were private comments to Russian president Vladimir Putin and German leader Gerhard Schröder. Speaking about their mutual allies the British, Chirac said, "The only thing they have ever done for European agriculture is mad cow disease." He added: "You cannot trust people who have such bad cuisine. It is the country with the worst food after Finland." Chirac thought the comments were private...but reporters overheard them. The next day the insults made headlines all over Europe—especially in the UK, where the British press savaged Chirac. (The *Sun* called him a "petty, racist creep.") Boycotts of French foods followed, and the insults caused serious tension between the two nations. Just two days after Chirac made the comments, the International Olympic Committee met to decide who would host the 2012 Olympics: London or Paris. Paris was the favorite, but London got the Games. How much it had to do with the two Finns on the final voting board, we'll never know for sure.

WORLDS WERE ROCKED

In the 1980s, Michael Jackson was certainly the most popular—and arguably the most recognizable—entertainer in the world. His 1982 album *Thriller* sold more than 42 million copies, his 1987 follow-up *Bad* sold 17 million, he pioneered the music video format, and he popularized the Moonwalk and the idea of wearing a single, sparkly glove.

His profile as both a musician and an icon dwindled in the 1990s because of Jackson's bizarre behavior and eccentric personal life. He attempted a comeback in 2001: He held a show at Madison Square Garden celebrating 30 years as a solo artist, and he recorded a new album, *Invincible*, with a top-10 hit, "You Rock My World," his first hit single in more than five years. He also hired a British film crew to follow him and his three children around and make a documentary about him.

But instead of lionizing the singer, the film made Jackson look alarmingly weird. *Living with Michael Jackson*, which aired in 2003 on ABC, depicted, among other things, Jackson dangling his infant son over a balcony and admitting to sleeping in beds with children. This led to Jackson's arrest on child abuse charges, a controversy that haunted his career from then on. Jackson never had another hit song, and died in 2009.

EXCERPTS FROM ACTUAL INSURANCE CLAIMS

Coming home I drove into the wrong house and collided with a tree I don't have."

• "The accident occurred when I was attempting to bring my car out of a skid by steering it into the other vehicle."

• "I was backing my car out of the driveway in the usual manner, when it was struck by the other car in the same place it had been struck several times before."

• "I bumped into a lamppost which was obscured by human beings."

• "I was driving along when I saw kangaroos copulating in the middle of the road causing me to ejaculate through the sun roof."

• "The car in front hit the pedestrian but he got up so I hit him again."

• "I knew the dog was possessive about the car but I would not have asked her to drive it if I had thought there was any risk."

• "My car was legally parked as it backed into another vehicle."

• "The other car collided with mine without giving warning of its intention."

- "I had been shopping for plants all day and was on my way home. As I reached an intersection a hedge sprang up obscuring my vision and I did not see the other car."

- "To avoid hitting the bumper of the car in front I struck a pedestrian."

- "First car stopped suddenly, second car hit first car, and a haggis ran into the rear of second car."

- "As I approached an intersection a stop sign suddenly appeared in a place where no stop sign had ever appeared before."

- "Windshield broken. Cause unknown. Probably voodoo."

- "I was sure the old fellow would never make it to the other side of the road when I struck him."

- "No one was to blame for the accident but it would never have happened if the other driver had been alert."

- "I started to slow down, but the traffic was more stationary than I thought."

- On approach to the traffic lights, the car in front suddenly broke.

- "I thought my window was down but I found it was up when I put my head through it."

- "I didn't think the speed limit applied after midnight."

YOU SHOULDN'T BE NAKED

In May 2007, British bride-groom Stephen Mallone, 25, was celebrating a stag weekend in Bratislava, Slo-vakia, when he decided it would be good fun to strip naked and swim in a public fountain. He was arrested and sentenced to two months in jail—which meant he would be missing his £20,000 wed-ding. After nearly two weeks, Slovakian authorities finally relented—and Mr. Mallone made it to the church on time.

• A man from Cookeville, Tennessee, visited the local mall. When he returned to his car, it wouldn't start. A heavy rainstorm came through and the man, not wanting to get mud on his car's seat covers via muddy and wet clothes, stripped naked before he got underneath the car to diagnose the problem. That's when police arrived and arrested him for indecent exposure. The charge was later dropped, but not until after he was fired from his job as an industrial engineer.

GARFIELD HATES MONDAYS, VETERANS

Since 1978, Jim Davis has drawn and authored *Garfield*, one of the most popular daily comic strips in the world. He works in advance, sending out finished *Garfield* episodes to his syndicate and newspapers as much as a year ahead of time.

This strip ran in November 2010: Garfield the cat holds up a rolled newspaper about to squish a spider. The spider implores him to stop, saying, "If you squish me, I shall become famous! They will hold an annual day of remembrance in my honor, you fat slob!" The final panel depicts a classroom full of spiders, with a spider teacher asking "Does anyone here know why we celebrate National Stupid Day?" The implication is that Garfield killed the spider, and that he was stupid for baiting the cat.

The strip, celebrating "National Stupid Day," ran in newspapers on Veterans Day. Davis issued an apology, saying he didn't know the strip would run on Veterans Day, and called it "the worst timing ever."

THAT SINKING FEELING

April 15, 2012, was the 100th anniversary of the sinking of the *Titanic*. Former baseball star and reality TV show participant José Canseco thought he'd tweet some thoughts:

• "Titanic 100 years wow. Global warming could've saved titanic. Sad to say."

• "Because we don't recycle and consume like crazy icicles are non existent. Titanic would've still existed today." ("Icicles" apparently referred to "icebergs," which, by the way, do exist.)

• "With global warming the weather is hotter so the icebergs would be melted and titanic saved."

• "Titanic reminds me of the days I had two yachts in Miami," he wrote, "but no icicles."

NICE MOVE, SLICK

CHOKING HAZARD
Millions of cute animals got an unwanted oil bath, all because Captain Joe Hazelwood got drunk and went to bed. Yet was the 1989 Exxon *Valdez* oil spill really caused by a lone drunk man? That's what the Exxon Shipping Company's lawyers argued. In court, Hazelwood admitted that in the hours preceding the accident, he and a few other officers had had a few vodkas in the town of Valdez, Alaska, where the ship had been docked. By the time they arrived back onboard that evening, Hazelwood claimed, he was sober. He took command, and the 986-foot tanker carrying 53 million gallons of crude oil departed for California. After being guided out of the Narrows by a tugboat, the *Valdez* had to navigate its way out of the rocky Prince William Sound. Captain Hazelwood had successfully performed this maneuver many times.

MIDNIGHT OIL
It was a "dark and misty" night, and the ship's sonar had picked up ice floating on the surface. Hazelwood plotted a new course outside of the regular shipping lanes to avoid the ice. He then asked Third Mate Greg Cousins, "Do you feel comfortable enough that I can go below and get

rid of some paperwork?" Cousins said he was. He was authorized to take command of the ship in open waters, but he did not have a license to pilot the ship in difficult Prince William Sound. But Hazelwood had confidence in him. So he went to his cabin to "sleep off his bender," as newspapers would later report. Cousins took control and spouted off orders to helmsman Robert Kagan, who was on his first ocean voyage in four years.

There was more ice on the water than Cousins expected and, according to Kagan, at one point Cousins became "panicked" and ordered Kagan to take a hard right. Kagan refused. Cousins then tried to take the wheel himself. Kagan refused to let him. Barely 10 minutes after he got to his cabin, Hazelwood received a call from Cousins: "We're getting into serious trouble here."

"Where's the rudder?" asked Hazelwood. But before Cousins could answer, at 12:04 a.m. on March 24, 1989, the Exxon *Valdez* ran aground on an underwater rock formation called Bligh Reef. Hazelwood hung up and ran to the bridge. He took the helm and tried to free the ship from the jagged rocks. He made the problem worse. Within a few hours, eight of the ship's 11 cargo tanks had ruptured, and about 11 million gallons of crude had gushed out into the sea.

YOU'RE SOAKING IN IT
As the spill made international headlines, Captain Hazelwood became the scapegoat. News programs showed globules of crude oil washing

up along 1,300 miles of Alaska's pristine southern coastline. It covered everything it came in contact with—orcas, herring, salmon, seals, birds, otters, clams, even plankton.

"THE COMPANY'S LAWYERS' MAIN ARGUMENT: EXXON DIDN'T DO IT ON PURPOSE, SO IT SHOULDN'T BE PUNISHED AS IF IT DID."

To this day, crude oil from the *Valdez* can be found in Prince William Sound, and the region's tourism and fishing industry never completely rebounded. The *Valdez* accident wasn't even in the top 50 spills in terms of the amount of oil lost, but it has become one of the most infamous manmade disasters of all time.

DISORDER IN THE COURT

A judge initially fined the company $5 billion, equal to one year's profits. Exxon appealed and got the amount reduced. Then it appealed again... and again—each time getting the amount whittled down even more. The company's lawyers' two main arguments: 1) Exxon didn't do it on purpose, so it shouldn't be punished as if it did; and 2) If Captain Hazelwood hadn't gotten drunk and left the bridge, the ship wouldn't have crashed.

Exxon took the case all the way to the U.S. Supreme Court. In 2008 eight of the nine judges heard oral arguments. (Justice Samuel Alito recused himself because he owns Exxon stock.) The court's ruling: Exxon's actions were "worse than negligent but less than malicious." They reduced the punitive damages from $2.5 billion to $500 million.

Third Mate Greg Cousins was cleared of all charges. Captain Hazelwood was acquitted of felony charges but found guilty of a misdemeanor "negligent discharge of oil." He was fined $50,000 and sentenced to 1,000 hours of community service. He never captained a ship again.

UNSOUND POLICIES

According to BBC journalist Greg Palast, who spent much of the 1990s investigating the accident, executives at Exxon, British Petroleum, and other oil companies were to blame, as they knew of the risks of a spill in Prince William Sound. After all, that's where the Alaska Pipeline lets out, and it would have been far too costly to move operations to a less fragile area. So for more than a decade, charged Palast, the companies falsified records, threatened whistleblowers with blackmail, and cut safety costs.

Here's the worst part: The *Valdez* disaster could have been prevented by a piece of radar-repeating equipment called the RAYCAS (Raytheon Collision Avoidance System). Unlike the ship's sonar, the RAYCAS could detect objects underwater. "The third mate," said Palast, "would never have hit Bligh Reef had he simply looked at his RAYCAS radar. But he could not. Why? Because it was not turned on. The complex system costs a lot to operate, so frugal Exxon management left it broken and useless."

THE ULTIMATE ZIPPER ACCIDENT

Phillip Seaton of Waddy, Kentucky, had gone to the hospital in 2007 to be circumcised, in order to better treat an inflammatory problem. During the procedure, however, Seaton's physician, Dr. John Patterson, discovered that Seaton's penis was, as he later testified, "riddled with cancer." So what did Dr. Patterson do? He lopped it off.

When Seaton came to, he was, reasonably, very upset to find out that his penis was gone, and had been removed without his consent. He sued Dr. Patterson, claiming that he never gave permission to have his penis cut off and was not given the opportunity to get a second opinion.

"This case isn't about a man's penis being removed," Dr. Patterson's lawyer said in court, "it's about cancer being removed." Seaton's lawyer argued that his client should have had the opportunity to treat the cancer in such a way that it require the lopping off of his penis.

The judge initially sided with the doctor; the case is currently under appeal. But no matter what happens, or however much money Seaton gets in a settlement, he'll never get his penis back. But he doesn't have cancer, which is nice.

UNCLE JOHN'S BATHROOM READER CLASSIC SERIES

Find these and other great titles from the Uncle John's Bathroom Reader Classic Series at *www.bathroomreader.com*.

Or contact us at:
Bathroom Readers' Institute
P.O. Box 1117
Ashland, OR 97520
(888) 488-4642

THE LAST PAGE

FELLOW BATHROOM READERS:

The fight for good bathroom reading should never be taken loosely—
we must do our duty and sit firmly for what we believe in, even while
the rest of the world is taking potshots at us.

We'll be brief. Now that we've proven we're not simply a
flush-in-the-pan, we invite you to take the plunge:

Sit Down and Be Counted! Log on to www.bathroomreader.com
and earn a permanent spot on the BRI honor roll!

....

If you like reading our books...
VISIT THE BRI'S WEBSITE!
www.bathroomreader.com

- Visit "The Throne Room"—a great place to read!
- Receive our irregular newsletters via e-mail
- Order additional *Bathroom Readers*
- Face us on Facebook
- Tweet us on Twitter
- Blog us on our blog

Go with the Flow...

....

Well, we're out of space, and when you've gotta go,
you've gotta go. Tanks for all your support.
Hope to hear from you soon.

Meanwhile, remember...

KEEP ON FLUSHIN'!